WHAT PAINTER
COULD EVER CAPTURE THIS?

Mountain Market, Clearing Mist, leaf from an album on the popular theme "Eight Views of the Xiao and Xiang" (瀟湘八景) by Xia Gui (Hsia Kuei 夏珪, active ca. 1195–1230), Metropolitan Museum of Art, John Stewart Kennedy Fund, 1913, 13.100.102. A popular subject in painting and poetry, the rivers are mentioned in poems 28, 48, 73, and 175.

WHAT PAINTER COULD EVER CAPTURE THIS?

Poetry of the Four Lings of Song China

Translated and Introduced by
Jonathan Chaves

FLOATING WORLD EDITIONS

First edition, 2023

Published by Floating World Editions

Some poems were previously published as noted.
Cover shows seals carved by Qi Baishi, inspired by poem 69. See note on page 83.

Printed in the USA

ISBN 978-1-953225-05-4

CONTENTS

To Jonathan Cott,
author, editor, interviewer,
brilliant reader of Chinese poetry in translation,
and friend

Editorial Notes

Although the pinyin system of rendering Chinese will be used throughout this book, existing titles and quotes from earlier sources will adhere to the romanization systems originally used, and Wade-Giles equivalents of major figures will be given on first mention. Unless p (for page number) is indicated, cross-references refer to poem numbers.

Contemporary painting of the Four Lings by Dai Honghai (戴宏海 b. 1941).
Although which Ling is which is not indicated, chances are that they are
arranged top to bottom, right to left, as named in the inscription: upper-right,
Xu Zhao (徐照); lower-right, Xu Ji (徐璣); upper-left, Weng Juan (翁卷);
lower-left, Zhao Shixiu (趙師秀). The complete inscription by Xiu Jiandan
(休劍丹), is translated opposite.

The Four Lings of Yongjia

"The Four Lings of Yongjia are Southern Song Dynasty poets Xu Zhao (Linghui 靈暉), Xu Ji (Lingyuan 靈淵), Weng Juan (Lingshu 靈舒), and Zhao Shixiu (Lingxiu 靈秀). The courtesy name of each includes the word *ling* [numinous]. What is more, the poetic tone of the four is quite similar, and their styles are close. All four are men of Yongjia, hence they are called The Four Lings of Yongjia. They all base their poetic styles on poets of the Late Tang. Their diction is exquisitely crafted, pure and elegant, placid and serene, while they depict nature imagery with impeccable precision. In the poetic world of the Southern Song they established themselves as a unique school and those who followed their style during that period were very numerous."

—inscription by Xiu Jiandan

INTRODUCTION

The poetry of the Song Dynasty (960–1279) has come to be fairly well known among aficionados of Chinese poetry in the West. This has mostly been due to a series of books on individual Song poets, beginning with three volumes that all appeared in 1946 and 1947: Gerald Bullett, *The Golden Year of Fan Ch'eng-ta* (Cambridge University Press, 1946); Clara M. Candlin, *The Rapier of Lu—Patriot Poet of China* (London: John Murray, 1946; Candlin had also published a general anthology of Song poetry entitled *The Herald Wind* with the same publisher in 1933); and Lin Yutang, *The Gay Genius: The Life and Times of Su Tungpo* (New York: John Day, 1947), this last one of the fullest studies of an individual Chinese poet ever published in English.

Later books by Burton Watson and others would expand the available corpus of Song poetry in translation, and Watson's translation in 1967 of *An Introduction to Sung Poetry*, first published in 1962 by the great Japanese scholar, Yoshikawa Kōjirō (translation by Harvard University Press, 1967), provided an excellent overall history of the subject. The emphasis in all these books was on the classic *shi* 詩, with even line lengths throughout an individual poem (usually five or seven characters), quite appropriately, because as Yoshikawa himself pointed out, the *shi* remained by far the most important and prestigious genre in Chinese poetry throughout dynastic history, while the *ci* 詞 or "lyric" type, with its uneven line lengths following established "tune-patterns," also achieved a high level of accomplishment in the Song and has also been introduced in numerous books and articles.

The poets introduced by Bullett and Candlin were two of the so-called "Four Masters of Southern Song Poetry," Fan Chengda (Fan Ch'eng-ta 范成大, 1126–91) and Lu Yu (Lu You 陸游, 1125–1210), to whom should be added the name of the third great master of this group, Yang Wan-li (Yang Wanli 楊萬里, 1127–1206)—the identity of the fourth shifting with time and never associated with a writer of equal importance to the other three. Yang has been introduced to Western readers in books by J.D. Schmidt—*Yang Wan-li* (Boston: Twayne, 1976), and myself—*Heaven My Blanket, Earth My Pillow: Poems from Sung China by Yang Wan-li* (Tokyo: Weatherhill, 1975; new edition, Buffalo: White Pine Press, 2004). Schmidt has also given us a fuller study of Fan Chengda—*Stone Lake: The Poetry of Fan Chengda* (Cambridge University Press, 1992), and Watson has provided two additional collections of poems and prose writings by Lu Yu—*The Old Man Who Does As He Pleases* (Columbia University Press, 1973), and *Late Poems of Lu You, The Old Man Who Does As He Pleases* (Tokyo and Toronto: ahadada books, 2007).

The view of Chinese poetic history thus presented to Western readers, and in fact already taken for granted by Chinese and Japanese readers as well, has been that with these Southern Song masters, Song poetry essentially came to an end, to be followed by later developments in the last three dynasties: the Yüan (1279–1368), Ming (1368–1644), and Qing (1644–1911). Such a view, however, leaves out of consideration a number of quite accomplished poets in the later Song Dynasty, whose work is deserving of closer attention both because of its innate quality, and because of its key role as a bridge to the later history of Chinese poetry.

Among the most important of the late Song poets were four men from Yongjia 永嘉, an alternate name for the city of Wenzhou 溫州 on the Zhejiang seacoast. They were known as the "Four Lings" 四靈 because, apparently by common consent, they all had *noms-de-plume* containing the character *ling*, meaning "numinous" or "magical." The four were: Weng Juan[1] (Weng Chüan 翁卷, d. after 1214), Xu Zhao (Hsü Chao 徐照, d. 1211), Xu Ji (Hsü Chi 徐璣, 1162–1214), and Zhao Shixiu (Chao Shih-xiu 趙師秀, 1170–1219). Since only Zhao Shixiu and

---

[1] His personal name can also be read as Quan (Ch'üan). For more on Weng, see Jonathan Chaves, *West Cliff Poems: The Poetry of Weng Chüan* (Tokyo and Toronto: ahadada books, 2010).

Xu Ji ever held minor official posts for brief periods of time, the four are called "citizen poets" by Yoshikawa, that is, individuals who were townsmen—usually merchants—or landowners in the countryside. As Yoshikawa shows, the emergence of poets among such circles, with only slight precedent in the earlier Song Dynasty, was a new movement in the late Song, indicating a "popularization" of poetry, which he further compares to developments that would occur in Japan's Edo period (1603–1868). At the same time, it should be kept in mind that these men, as noted, did sometimes serve briefly in official capacity, and, more importantly, maintained close relations with other scholar-official literati, so that it is possible to overstate the distinction between the two groups.

Some continuity with the previous generation of poets is indicated by the fact that Xu Ji, at least, addressed a poem to Yang Wanli, who was to die in 1206. The poem is reverential in tone, but emphasizes Yang's stature as a Confucian literatus (*ru* 儒) rather than his influence as a poet. Still, there can be no doubt that the Four Lings, while certainly looking to the late Tang period for inspiration, as noted by most students of their work, learned a good deal as well from Yang and the other Southern Song masters who preceded them.

One of the most important writers to follow the Four Lings, and himself a giant of late Song literature and a superb literary critic, Liu Kezhuang (Liu K'o-chuang 劉克莊, 1187–1269), wrote a poem for Weng Juan, laying out what amounts to his critique of all the Four Lings:[2]

> *Presented to Weng Juan*
> Not only master of Tang Dynasty style,
> but especially skilled at the *Anthology* mode.
> At times, affairs sweeping a thousand years

---

[2] The poem will be found in Liu's collected works, *Hou cunji* 後村集 (edition of the Siku Quanshu 四庫全書), 7/6b.

are encompassed in just one of your couplets.
Men of this age look lightly on their forerunners,
But Heaven has injected life into this Old Man!
If among the lakes and rivers I do not encounter you,
I'll surely see you somewhere, east or west.

Liu here praises Weng, while punning on his surname, which also means "Old Man," or "Venerable Gentleman." He grants Weng a reputation as a reviver of Tang style at a time when contemporaries do not give it sufficient respect, while further praising his ability to write in the manner of the *Literary Anthology* (*Wenxuan* 文選), the single most influential anthology of pre-Tang literature, compiled between the years 526 and 531, according to Jao Tsung-i.[3] This is high praise from an important cultural arbiter in late Song China. And yet most critics, starting from their own day, would tend to take a narrower view of Weng and the other Lings. Characteristic of what would become the standard view of their work, even by their admirers, would be the comment of Zhao Ruhui (Chao Ju-hui 趙汝回), a minor poet who obtained his *chin-shih* degree in 1214 while Weng Juan was almost certainly still alive:

> The Tang style was not being kept vibrant; exist-
> ing schools of poets derived their lineage from the
> Jiangxi school. It was the Four Lings of Yongjia who
> first made it their goal to match themselves against
> the Kaiyuan [713–740] and Yuanhe [806–820] mas-
> ters [i.e., the so-called High and Mid-Tang poets,
> the greatest of the Tang dynasty]. They refined and
> polished their work until every single word rang
> out like jade. If you were to mix their works in with

---

[3] Rao Zongyi (饒宗頤, 1917–2018). See his entry on the *Wenxuan* in William H. Nienhauser, Jr., et al, *The Indiana Companion to Traditional Chinese Literature* (Indiana University Press, 1986), p. 891.

those of Yao and Jia, no one would be able to distin-
guish them.[4]

Yao and Chia were Yao He (Yao Ho 姚合, fl. 831) and Jia Dao
(Chia Tao 賈島, 779–843),[5] generally considered to represent what in
the Song dynasty was called the "Late Tang" style, characterized by
relatively small-scale, exquisitely described nature scenes, usually in
the form of five-character per line "regulated verse" poems of eight
lines, the type indeed favored by the Four Lings. It is clear that, while
Zhao is praising these poets, in fact he sees their achievement as
modest by comparison with their purpose: they may have wished to
revive the great Tang style, but settled for the lesser delights of "Late
Tang," and specifically Yao He and Jia Dao, whose work—in particu-
lar Jia's—was indeed of great importance to them. Zhao is impatient
with the preference of most of the contemporaries of the Four Lings
for sticking with the established Song lineage of the Jiangxi school.
His idea that the Lings brought new freshness into Chinese poetry by
reaching *back* to the past for inspiration is in keeping with the idea
of "Reviving antiquity" (*fugu* 復古) as a form of *revitalization*. We may
think of the comparable recurring phenomenon in Western literary
history: Neo-Classicism, the Romantics with their nostalgia for a lost
classical or medieval past, the Preraphaelites, etc. And for both East
and West, it is not mere imitation which is at work, but a quest for a
new stimulus from the past.

Other critics, again almost from the first, held what they saw as
the narrowness of the Four Lings' style against them. A key critique,

---

[4] Zhao's comment is cited by Li E (厲鶚, 1692–1752), *Songshi jishi* 宋詩紀事 (edition published by Shanghai Guji Chubanshe in two vols., 1983), Vol. II, p. 1583. See p. 2059 of the same work for Zhao Juhui.

[5] For translations from Jia Dao, see Mike O'Connor trans., *When I Find You Again, It Will Be in Mountains* (Wisdom Publications, 2000). For more on the Late Tang style as here defined, see Jonathan Chaves, *Mei Yao-ch'en and the Development of Early Sung Poetry* (Columbia University Press, 1976), pp. 53–59.

perhaps the first, of this type is this one by Fan Xiwen (Fan Hsi-wen 范晞文) from his book of poetic criticism, *Nighttime Discussions from Facing Beds* (*Dui chuang yeyu*, 對牀夜語), a book whose preface is dated 1262:

> The Four Lings were men who championed "Tang" poetry. If we seek out the best of them, it was probably Zhao Shixiu. But those possessed of real insight will consider that even he did not really complete the task. For we must regret that these poets *did not set their sights high enough, but limited themselves to Yao and Chia* [emphasis added].

Fan goes on to lament that their followers, while trying to expand on their work, actually fell to a still lower level. His singling out of Zhao Shixiu as probably the best of the four is echoed by other writers.[6]

Such harshness should not surprise us, as there is a long-standing tradition of strongly worded advocacy and opposition in Chinese poetic criticism. Those who have particularly come in for negative critiques have been precisely those who have tended towards the relatively realistic, smaller scale approach employed by the Late Tang poets, as well as their emulators, the late Song poets—that is, the Four Lings. Such poets also leaned toward understated, straightforward diction that incurred the enmity of those who preferred a more flowery, allusive style. The whole history of Chinese poetry, in fact, can be seen as driven by an interesting tension between these two tendencies. It might also be noted that some of Weng's poems dealing with the quest for immortality do indeed have some of the grandiosity associated with such a High Tang poet as Li Bai (Li Po 李白, 701–62).

The Four Lings must thus be seen as continuing and breathing new

---

6 See the edition published by Ding Fubao, *Xu lidai shihua* 續歷代詩話 (reprint by Yiwen yinshu guan), Vol. II, 2/2a.

life into the stream of poetic style finding its ultimate source in the great Tao Qian (T'ao Ch'ien 陶潛, 365–427), reaching a further peak in the work of Bai Juyi (Po Chü-i 白居易, 772–846), and deliberately cultivated to provide a basis for a new Song dynasty poetry by Mei Yaochen (Mei Yao-ch'en 梅堯臣, 1002–60) and his protégé, the supreme Song-Dynasty poet, Su Shi, aka Su Dongpo (Su Shih 蘇軾 also Su Tung-p'o 蘇東坡, 1037–1101), the subject of Lin Yutang's book, *The Gay Genius*. In Yang Wanli, this style reached yet another stage of development, and the Four Lings can be interpreted as keeping alive a version of this approach to poetry, allowing it in turn to bear further fruit in the future. Such poetry is immensely attractive to the modern poetry lover, and we must not be put off by the kinds of negative comments that routinely were aimed at such writing, in the case of the Four Lings by Fan Xiwen, as we have seen. Without its leavening influence, Chinese poetry could easily have degenerated into a highly bookish or pedantic craft little related to the world of actual human experience.

In praising Weng Juan, Liu Kezhuang used the remarkable phrase, "Heaven has *injected life* into this 'Weng'" 天猶活此翁. Liu may have had in mind the term *huo-fa* 活法, "lively method," sometimes applied to the poetry of Yang Wanli. Yang, influenced by Chan (Zen) Buddhist ideas of "sudden enlightenment," especially in his quatrains, likes to give mini-enlightenment experiences to his readers, as in "Passing the Pavilion on Shenzhu Bridge:"[7]

> I get down from my palanquin,
>> and look around the country inn.
> I'm surprised by the cold sound of water beneath my feet.
> The Yangzi River is closer than I thought:
> Suddenly, above the bamboo grove,
>> an inch of mast floats by.

[7] Translation from Jonathan Chaves, *Heaven My Blanket, Earth My Pillow: Poems from Sung Dynasty China by Yang Wan-li* (Buffalo: White Pine Press, 2004), p. 60.

The poet is standing on a bridge, and is surprised by the intensity of the flow of water beneath, unexpected for a sleepy stream. But, "suddenly"—a favorite word of Yang's (*hu* 忽 or *huran* 忽然), a seemingly inconsequential, everyday occurrence leads to heightened awareness, an expansion of vision and knowledge: above a bamboo grove which he had presumably considered to belong to an on-going forest, he sees a bit of the *mast* of a boat moving along, and in a flash he knows that the mighty Yangzi River is close by! Thus an everyday experience becomes a kind of microcosm of the full Chan enlightenment experience, or rather, is equivalent to it.

This delightful and very effective "lively method" of Yang's is rarely emulated by later writers, requiring as it does a very specific kind of consciousness. But in poem 65 of this collection, Zhao comes very close to Yang's mode of playfulness:

> *Several Days*
> For several days, the autumn wind
>   has cheated this sick man:
> It's blown down all the yellow leaves,
>   into the courtyard weeds.
> The woods once sparse, they would allow
>   far mountains to appear,
> When—no! Again they're half concealed
>   as clouds come drifting through.

Just as we think we're going to get a clear few of the once foliage-veiled distant mountains, we're tricked by the sudden appearance of inward drifting clouds! Those critics who have sneered at poetry of this sort have failed to grasp the great paradox that the *simple* can be the *profound*; just as, of course, the *complex* can sometimes turn out to be merely *superficial*.

It comes as no surprise, therefore, to find a great many references in Zhao's poetry to Buddhist monks who were friends of his, while at the same time, like others of the Four Lings, it is clear that he has great admiration for recluses and retired scholars of every description. For example, in poem 66 he visits a Daoist practitioner in a very remote location:

> *At Night Returning to Jade Purity Shrine*
> Before the cliff, the cassia blossoms
>   haven't opened yet;
> I've come to seek out in this shrine
>   the Daoist Master here.
> As light rain falls, the pine tree road
>   turns completely dark . . .
> But—fireflies suddenly come flying out,
>   illumining blue-green lichens.

The general numinousness of the recluse's place of retirement is indicated by the sudden appearance of the magical fireflies illuminating lichens.

The retirement of the recluse in this poem echoes the theme as it runs through so many of the poems of all Four Lings. In fact, a dichotomy between "going forth" to serve in the civil service bureaucracy, and "withdrawing" to some degree of reclusive retirement, is so essential in Chinese thought that it may be considered a timeless component of Chinese civilization. Nor is it a merely "Daoist" as opposed to "Confucian" concept; Confucius himself famously declares in his *Analects* (7:11): "When they make use of you, then act; when they reject you, then hide away." 用之則行，舍之則藏. He is speaking to Yan Hui 顏回, his favorite disciple. To "hide away" (*cang* 藏) implies withdrawal and reclusion of some kind, but with a readiness to re-emerge to serve, when the times improve. The dynamic of choice between these two courses of action will therefore run throughout traditional Chinese history, and will constitute a perennial theme in poetry.

The Four Lings in their actual lives, aside from occasional low-level service in the administrations of local officials, were living outside the world of officialdom, while not yet participating in the full reclusion they so admired. They were *buyi* 布衣, "men in plain clothes," fully educated literati but not pursuing government service. There is an undoubted tension between service and withdrawal of various degrees and types, but it is a healthy one, encompassing a full and complex view of human life.

The Four Lings deserve to be considered poets of consequence. Zhao and Weng are the most frequently cited in the writings of traditional scholars, and are therefore more profusely represented here, although the two Xu's are also excellent. Indeed, it would be nearly impossible to convincingly distinguish amongst them stylistically. It is almost as if they share one poetic sensibility.

Those literati critics who were suspicious of *simplicity*—often equating it with "commonness," even "vulgarity" (*su* 俗), going so far as to apply it to the great Bai Juyi himself in many cases—were on one side of a divide of longstanding in the rich history of Chinese poetic criticism, privileging poetry dense with allusions, sometimes in nearly every line. The Four Lings might counter that these critics are themselves are tainted by pedantry or bookishness in their own poetic work.

Painting by Liu Yu (Liu Yü 劉育, 1620–after 1689) incorporating the penulti-
mate couplet from *The Melon Hut of Xue Shishi* (see poem 27), courtesy of
the National Museum of Asian Art, Smithsonian Institution, Arthur M. Sackler
Collection, Gift of Arthur M. Sackler, S1987.227.10 27.

72 POEMS BY ZHAO SHIXIU

(Lingxiu 靈秀, 1170–1219)

Page numbers refer to the Chinese texts in the one-chapter collected works of Zhao Shixiu, "Poetry Collection from the Studio of the Garden of Purity" (*Qingyuan zhai shiji* 清苑齋詩集) in the *Siku quanshu* (四庫全書). Poems 1 through 5 were translated for Charles Rossiter, and first appeared in *Big Scream* (Nada Press, 59, 2020).

1 | At Willow Embankment—Sent to Xu Zhao

It's poverty has kept us far apart;
Already I've done thirteen treks.
The whole day I walk through mountain scenes,
And meeting someone, ask, "What place is this?"
I've written letters, but have no way to send them.
With whom else can I discuss new poems?
I picture you, in the rains of this cold night.
Are you thinking of me? Dreaming of me?

Xu Zhao is a fellow member of the Four Lings.

楊柳塘寄徐照　　　　　　p. 5b

因貧為遠別; 已是十三程
盡日行山色; 逢人問地名
近書無便寄; 新句與誰評
想爾寒宵雨; 思予亦夢成

24

2 | Presented to Kong, Master of the Dao

Born with Confucius's surname!
Why aren't you wearing scholar's robe and cap?
Your poems are good—you chant them to visitors;
Your lute, crystal clear—but you play only for yourself.
To call on you, I walked from the distant town,
Loved passing through cool bamboo around your hermitage.
They tell me for you it's no problem
To turn the cinnabar in the brazier into gold!

The poet humorously notes the irony that even though his friend bears the surname of China's greatest sage, Confucius (Kong Fuzi 孔夫子) he seems more interested in Daoist alchemy than literati pursuits (see 74). Turning cinnabar into gold would be evidence of masterly alchemical skills.

贈孔道士 pp. 5b–6a

生來還姓孔；何不戴儒冠
詩好逢人誦；琴清只自彈
訪師行郡遠；愛竹透庵寒
見説丹爐内；黄金化不難

3 | TRAVELING BY BOAT–SENT TO WENG THE TENTH

In this light skiff, the wind is just perfect
Skimming waves farther and farther away.
I take out your poems, and reread them—
They cure me of the illnesses I have!
River birds rest on evening trees;
Streams merge in, swelling the autumn tide.
Already, I feel I miss you awfully,
Yet since we parted, just a single day!

Weng the Tenth is Weng Juan, a fellow member of the Four Lings.

舟行寄翁十　　　　　　　p. 6b

輕舟風色好; 波面去迢迢
取爾詩重讀; 令吾病欲銷
江禽停晚樹; 澗水入秋潮
已覺懷人極; 分攜始一朝

4 | A MONK AT STONE GATE

Stone Gate is incredibly remote;
There you live alone, just one Zen monk.
The temple, abandoned, but the bell remains;
Walls rise high, visitors can climb up.
The wild mountain bees make a bitter honey;
The waterfall stops frozen halfway down.
Especially in such a frigid winter,
Who but you could possibly live here?

石門僧　　　　　　　　　p. 8b

石門幽絕甚; 獨有一禪僧
寺廢餘鐘在; 房高過客登
山蜂成苦蜜; 崖溜結空冰
如此冬寒月; 他人住豈能

5 | At Soul Mountain Pavilion Viewing the Old Inscribed Poems of my Friends, the Two Xu's

On one side, I see the stream;
All the other three are blue-green mountains.
I've come here late, and beyond deserted railings
Autumn approaches as white clouds fly.
My second visit, just as my body's aging
I'm sad my fellow-poets are not here.
Soul Mountain, naturally like a painting,
Just as before, screening the setting sun.

The "Two Xu's" addressed are fellow Four Lings, Xu Zhao and Xu Ji.

靈山閣見二徐友舊題句　　　pp. 8b–9a

一面見溪水；三邊皆翠微
晚來虛檻外；秋近白雲飛
重至恰身老；同吟感客非
靈山自如畫；依舊隔斜暉

6 | THE SHRINE OF PAULOWNIAS AND CEDARS

Deep in the mountains, ground suddenly levels off;
Mist parts to reveal an unexpected courtyard.
A waterfall nearby, the spring breeze is all moist;
Pine trees everywhere, dawn sunlight glows green.
On a stone dais, a few crane-feathers lie;
On a white-washed wall, fragments of painted dragons.
The Daoist Master Wang Lingbao
Is light of foot, strong, a hundred years of age.

桐柏觀   p. 5b

山深地忽平; 縹緲見殊庭
瀑近春風濕; 松多曉日青
石壇遺鶴羽; 粉壁剝龍形
道士王靈寶; 輕強滿百齡

7 | STAYING OVERNIGHT AT JINYUN COUNTY

An old friend, aware of long separation,
Takes the trouble to stop by, bringing wine.
This ancient town has little population;
The spring chill bites as night comes on.
Rains absorb fragrance from herbs in this garden for Immortals;
Candlelight flickers on ripples beneath the stone bridge.
It's borne in upon me how far I am from home;
I can't understand half the local dialect.

緝雲縣宿   p. 6a

親知因別久; 具酒勞經過
古邑居人少; 春寒入夜多
雨香仙地藥; 燭動石橋波
稍覺離家遠; 鄉音一半訛

8 | ON THE ROAD TO JINXIAN

Halfway through the month, encountering Plum Rains,
At first, sky clear, traveler's sadness melts away.
Songs of warblers trail over rustic waters;
Shadows of pines repose on young rice-sprouts.
I call a brief halt, to rest the sedan-bearers;
Stroll at leisure over the wood-plank bridge.
My whole life, I've not been much of a drinker:
I feel strangely guilty at the summons of the wineshop flag.

Plum Rains refers to a rainy season that extends from late May
through July in the solar calendar.

進賢道中　　　　　　pp. 6a–b

半月逢梅雨; 初晴客意消
鶯聲臨野水; 松影卧新苗
少憩休輿卒; 閒行過板橋
平生無飲分; 空愧酒旗招

9 | Sitting at Night by Cold Stream

All realms turn blue-green, deep and deeper;
The moon shines straight at me, above the peak.
The bell from the bell-tower, even more resonant beneath a clear sky;
Water in the pond seems deeper with the night.
Pure, serene—this is no human realm;
In midst of Void one sees the heart of Buddha.
But now I seek out my place to spend the night;
As wind starts up among the wood's pine trees.

According to Wei Chingzhi, editor of *Shiren yuxie* (*Jade Dust of the Poets*, a twelfth-century work of literary criticism), the poet originally used the words 更 ("even more") and 如 ("to seem") in the second couplet (in bold below), then later changed them to 聽 ("to hear") and 觀 ("to view") respectively, a great improvement according to Wei. But the translator finds the earlier choices to be more resonant and so follows the original text.

冷泉夜坐   p. 6b

衆境碧沈沈; 前峰月正臨
樓鐘晴**更**響; 池水夜**如**深
清淨非人世; 虛空見佛心
却尋來處宿; 風起古松林

10 | THE SHRINE OF EXTENDED JOY

How desolate, this old palace for the Immortals!
Wind is always howling through the pine forest.
Crane-feathers mix with leaves in falling;
Well-vapors merge with the clouds.
Away from sunlight, moss-mottled bricks turn purplish;
The white-washed walls, so old, have no paintings left.
They say that Magistrate Tao Yuanming
Once resided among these mountains.

Tao Yuanming, also known as Tao Qian (T'ao Yuan-ming 陶淵明, 365–427) famously quit his official position as magistrate to return to his farmlands, see illustration on p. 88. As perhaps the most well-known scholar-recluse-poet, he is referred to by all of the Four Lings, see especially poem 78.

延禧觀   p. 7a

寂寞古仙宫；松林常有風
鶴毛兼葉下；井氣與雲同
背日苔磚紫；多年粉壁空
相傳陶縣令；曾住此山中

11 | LEANING ON THE BALUSTRADE

Leaning on the balustrade, startled by the passing of the years,
I've lived here long; wonder what comes next?
In this water-country, flowers bloom earlier;
In spring, many people climb the city walls.
My illness makes me too lazy to write poems;
At leisure, I'm grateful that many visitors come.
I hear them speak of the situation at the border:
The sages of today strive for a policy of peace.

Throughout the Southern Song Dynasty, northern China as far
south as the River Huai was occupied by the alien Jin Dynasty,
established by the Jurchen Tungus, a nomadic people from the
north, followed by the Mongol-established Yuan Dynasty, beginning
its conquest of all of China and which would terminate in 1279.

撫欄

p. 7a

撫欄驚歲月；久住欲如何
水國花開早；春城人上多
病令詩懶作；閒喜客頻過
聽說邊庭事；時賢策在和

12 | PRESENTED TO MASTER DA OF THE WESTERN HALL

In autumn waters, a few stalks of lotus,
Just to the side of your residence.
By these you may penetrate the Principle of Serenity
No longer worrying about worldly *karma*.
Your old vow at last is now fully accomplished;
Your divine prescriptions you now have time to transcribe.
At leisure, I ask of the temples where you resided:
"They're all like a dream, lost in the haze."

The recipient is almost certainly a Buddhist monk, who, after living the cenobitic life in monasteries, has withdrawn to the life of a solitary hermit. An excellent candidate for Master Da would be Shi Daguan (Shih Ta-kuan 釋達觀, 1138–1212), like the poet a member of the Imperial Zhao clan.

贈達西堂   p. 7b

秋水數枝蓮；在師房一邊
固應通淨理；不復念生緣
舊願酬初滿；靈方許盡傳
閒詢曾住寺；如夢已茫然

13 | SEEING OFF TANG GAN

You can compose literature, and are enlightened as to Buddha Nature:
You formerly were the Buddhist monk, Huixiu.
To take the examinations you've come to the capital,
But for poetry, you visit rustics like me.
Where you live is just across the stream,
Yet suddenly, ten days gone by without seeing you!
Why suddenly announce you must go home?
Now a Confucian scholar, you've been appointed to office.

A Buddhist monk who left the monastic life to take the administrative examinations and become an official, Tang Gan must first visit his parents to honor them.

送湯干   pp. 7b–8a

能文兼悟性； 前是惠休身
為選來京邑； 因吟訪野人
所居纔隔水； 不見忽經旬
何事云歸速； 儒官拜敕新

14 | AUTUMN COLORS

This hidden man loves the autumn colors,
Simply because they suit poetic feeling.
No sooner has the first leaf fallen
Than I've already got several good couplets.
"Austere" would be my vinewood staff, so light;
"Coolness" I feel in my coarse-cloth robe, so thin.
Along the deserted path in front of my gate
This year, the chrysanthemums grow all by themselves.

秋色   p. 8a

幽人愛秋色; 祇為屬吟情
一片葉初落; 數聯詩已清
瘦便藤杖細; 涼覺葛衣輕
門外蕭蕭徑; 今年菊自生

15 | BRIEF EPISTLE TO MY FELLOW TRAVELER, WENG LINGSHU

After several clear days, many clusters of stream-stones;
Our boats proceed, bow to stern.
All day long we don't see each other,
As if you and I were on separate trips.
The waterbirds are mostly snowy white;
The rustic flutes now turn to autumn tunes.
You certainly are writing new verses:
The crystal stream must yield to them in purity.

Weng Linshu is Weng Juan, fellow member of the Four Lings.

簡同行翁靈舒   p. 8b

久晴灘磧衆; 舟楫後先行
終日不相見; 與君如各程
水禽多雪色; 野笛忽秋聲
必有新詩句; 溪流合讓清

16 | THE TEMPLE OF THE GRASS-ROBED MONK AT XINZHOU

Four or five stalks of lotus
Grow all alone in the abandoned pond.
It is difficult to meet the Grass-Robed Monk;
All we can see is an old stele where we sit.
Fragrant mist conjures up the glory days;
In poetic lines we record our journey here.
We want to ask, "Where's his pet crane in the moss?"
The tall pines of course have no idea.

This fine example of the "deserted temple" genre records a journey taken by the poet and his friend and fellow-poet Weng Juan to an old temple where, according to tradition, a lone monk, weaving himself a robe from wild grasses, sat in meditation for thirty years.

信州草衣寺   p. 8b

芙蕖四五枝; 寂寞在空池
難見草衣士; 空看宴坐碑
香烟思盛日; 詩句記遊時
欲問苔中鶴; 長松自不知

17 | SEEING OFF MONK HUI AS HE RETURNS FOR A STAY AT THE TEMPLE OF VOID PHENOMENA

Suddenly we hear of the invitation:
Your monk's staff of tin points into autumn wind
The temple lies in a cold city,
A county seat amidst rustic waters.
Worldly karma not completely shuffled off,
Your old lectures now you'll be able to complete.
I won't seek you out, only to part again:
For a floating cloud, leaving and staying are the same.

Monk Hui has received a formal invitation to return to a temple
where he had commenced, but not completed, a series of
lectures.

送輝上人再住空相   p. 9b

忽然聞受請; 鐵錫指秋風
寺在寒城裏; 州居野水中
生緣拋未盡; 舊講續應終
不用相尋別; 浮雲去住同

18 | A MONK LIVING ON A CLIFF

You open your front gate: you're atop a stone cliff!
All day long, few people climb this far.
A single bird flits past the chilly trees;
A few flowers sway with the blue-green vines.
To brew tea? Water from beneath the ice;
For incense? A scented lamp before Buddha.
I too am one who has escaped the race for fame:
What karma led me to be like this monk?

嚴居僧   pp. 10a–b

開扉在石層; 盡日少人登
一鳥過寒木; 數花搖翠藤
茗煎氷下水; 香炷佛前燈
吾亦逃名者; 何因似此僧

19 | ALONG THE MOAT

Far and near, folks' houses spread around;
Cross the bridge—the path leads to them all.
Through farmland, skinny horses walk;
At a shallow bank cluster waterbirds.
The place is tranquil—faint rippling of a stream;
The weather, cold—setting sunlight, red.
Were I not a low-level clerk,
I'd never think that I was in a city.

壕上   p. 10b

遠近人家住; 過橋路盡通
野田行瘦馬; 淺渚聚群鴻
地靜微泉響; 天寒落日紅
若非身作吏; 不道是城中

38

20 | ON A MOONLIT NIGHT, THINKING OF XU ZHAO

The whole courtyard is deep in moon-colors;
My heart is a thousand miles away.
The River Xiang is right here before me,
But, autumn wanderer, with whom will I chant poems?
As cold comes in, horns blow from city walls;
Light congeals, birds roost among bamboo.
I know for sure that you're not sleeping either:
It will be hard to seek you out in dream.

The title refers to Xu Zhao of the Four Lings.

月夜懷徐照　　　　　　p. 11a

月色一庭深；迢遙千里心
湘江連底見；秋客與誰吟
寒入吹城角；光凝宿竹禽
亦知同不寢；難得夢相尋

21 | Mourning the Death of Xu Linghui

When alive, poverty was no problem for you;
But you've died so early! This brings real sorrow.
In the world out there, there is plenty of gold,
But now in society, there'll be no good verses.
Your soul must be flowing off with the River Xiang,
Your fame will rise as high as the Wandering Immortal's.
You always were really fond of tea:
I'll plant a few bushes right beside your grave.

Xu Zhao (Linghui) died in 1211. The "Wandering Immortal" (浪仙) refers to Jia Dao, a favorite late-Tang poet of the Four Lings. Their style was largely modeled on his (see Introduction, p 16, and poem 83).

徐靈暉挽詞   p. 12a

在生貧不害; 早喪可嗟吁
天下黃金有; 人間好句無
魂應湘水去; 名與浪仙俱
平日惟躭茗; 墳前種幾株

22 | AT GREAT PEACE MOUNTAIN, STUDYING–
SENT TO MY CITY FRIENDS

This rustic man, nothing else weighing on him,
Gets to sit here in the deserted forest.
Again, days of spreading open the books;
Yet my mind not yet enlightened to the blue lotus.
With the ring of the bell, the mountain hall is tranquil;
Firefly reflections glitter in the deep stone-girt pool.
I dare not invite your fragrant shoes to tread here,
But if you have some time, couldn't you just stop by?

The "blue lotus" can refer to the essence of Buddha's teaching,
although the image is also used to represent incorrupt
Confucian officials.

太平山讀書寄城中諸友　　　　　p. 12a

野人無別事; 故得坐空林
黄卷還鋪日; 青蓮未悟心
鐸音山殿靜; 螢影石池深
不敢邀芳屐; 因閒儻一尋

23 | THE POOL OF THE GREAT DRAGON

A stream-branch plunges in the void:
What painter could ever capture this?
A high wind blows it into rain;
Low sunbeams shoot a rainbow right across.
A book from the western regions records
Only by the former dynasty was a path cut through.
And some folks claim, the dragon's gone away,
Moving his palace to some other hidden spot.

Dragons, residing in deep mountain pools or other bodies of
water, were venerated as deities controlling rainfall. They were
said to have changed location when prayers to them for rain (or
against excessive rainfall) repeatedly failed. For more on this, see
Jonathan Chaves, *Cave of the Immortals: The Poetry and Prose
of Bamboo-Painter Wen Tong* (1019–1079), Floating World Edi-
tions, 2017, *passim*.

The phrase *xiyu shu* 西域書 in line 5 could be the name of a spe-
cific book *Book of the Western Regions* or, more likely, a generic
reference to "book(s) from the Western Regions," including from
outside of China, possibly texts in Sanskrit (written in scripts such
as *siddham, devanagari*, etc.). The translation assumes the latter
meaning. There are several references in various works to a monk
who resided at the Yandang Mountains (雁蕩山), and of the Pool
of the Great Dragon, a famed waterfall in those mountains. The
Yandang Mountains are located near the poet's hometown of
Yongzhia, modern Wenzhou, in the *east* of China. The likelihood
is that the monk came from India, and either he or an associate
recorded his story in Sanskrit, later translated into Chinese. But
this is speculation.

大龍湫　　　　　　　p. 12a

一派落虛空; 如何畫得同
高風吹作雨; 低日射成虹
西域書曾說; 先朝路始通
或言龍已去; 幽處別為宮

24 | PRESENTED TO OLD MONK YUE

A single path penetrates deep into bamboo:
Here are your few pillars overlooking an old canal.
There is no one else here living with you,
So you're very happy that a guest has come by.
Your white hair is so long, it reaches your shoulders;
Fresh tea is brewed, green filling our cups.
You tell me, there are other temples outside your gate,
All being restored by old monks like you.

In the original text, there is an hiatus of one character at the end
of line 5; "shoulders" (*jian* 肩) is a reasonable guess for the
missing word.

贈約老   pp. 12b–13a

一徑入深竹; 數楹臨古溝
更無人共住; 極喜客來遊
白髮長垂肩; 新茶綠滿甌
自言門外寺; 皆是老僧修

25 | TEMPLE OF THE BLUE-GREEN CLIFF

The stone cliff is simply invisible,
Veiled by layers of blue-green color.
Spring rains arise from the pine needles;
Mountain winds tinkle the wind-chimes.
The stele is tough for rubbing: a craftsman wastes much ink;
The grasses are soft, green weaving a carpet beneath.
An old monk from Wu resides here;
He welcomes me, recalls that we have met before.

Ink-rubbings of the epigraphic inscriptions on stone stelae would
be taken by placing the paper over the inscribed area, then
tamping it with an ink-laden round pad. The difficulty here may
be that many of the characters are partially eroded or effaced
and difficult to capture by the rubbing technique. Such rubbings
are themselves highly prized as works of art. In some cases, the
stelae have disappeared or become completely effaced, so that
the rubbings are the only record of the calligraphy.

翠巖寺 p. 13a

石巖看不見; 翠色自重重
春雨生松葉; 山風響鐵鐘
碑頑工費墨; 草嫩綠添茸
住院吳僧老; 相迎憶舊逢

26 | SEEING OFF HUANG SHUXIANG TO PAY A CALL ON MR. YANG BOZI

I hear that you served in the military:
How did you manage to gain a scholar's cap?
You chant some of your new poems for me,
Show me the scars of arrow wounds on your body.
Rewards you declined, because of poverty;
You alleviate by getting drunk.
And now you take the shepherd's staff for Huzhou:
Surely you'll take pity on the cold scholars there.

The second couplet is remarkable in paralleling the signs of
Huang's new scholarly credentials with the physical signs of his
former military service. The poem describes a relatively rare
example of "career change" in traditional China.

送黃叔向謁楊伯　　　　　　　p. 13b

嘗聞事將壇；何得復儒冠
口誦新詩句；身呈舊箭瘢
賞因貧未受；愁擬醉相寬
當仗湖州牧；應憐志士寒

27 | THE MELON HUT OF XUE SHISHI

You give no thought to becoming a noble;
Serenely, you distance yourself from the world.
Only planting melons interests you,
Though you've also a penchant for reading books.
Out here in the wilds, there's more water than land;
Half the spring mountains are clouds!
As for me, I hate that I'm growing old:
In studying gardening, I'm way behind you.

Planting melons is a long-established allusion to a scholar who left
the world of officialdom to plant melons, in other words to engage
in a type of reclusion expressing itself in gardening. Xue Shishi
(Hsüeh Shih-shih 薛師石, 1178–1228) was himself a significant
poet in a style similar to that of the Four Lings, and a good friend
of theirs. He never once held official position. Zhao was in fact
eight years older than Xue.

薛師石瓜廬   pp. 13b–14a

不作封侯念; 悠然遠世紛
惟應種瓜事; 猶被讀書分
野水多於地; 春山半是雲
吾生嫌已老; 學圃未如君

28 | SEEING OFF XU DAOHUI ON A JOURNEY TO THE RIVER XIANG

Spring is ending, rains fall in torrents;
Spring cold lingers on your robe.
The man will go off in search of fragrant herbs;
The wild geese return, athwart the distant peak.
River Xiao flows in, broadening River Xiang;
Tang Dynasty stelae grow rarer now in Song.
You must know I expect you will inscribe
Your name and surname on all the cliffside huts.

Xu Daohui being seen off is Xu Zhao.

送徐道暉遊湘水　　　　　p. 14a

春盡雨霏霏；春寒猶在衣
人尋香草去；鴈背遠峰歸
瀟水添湘闊；唐碑入宋稀
應知名與姓；題寫遍巖扉

29 | THE MOUNTAIN RESIDENCE OF HERMIT LIU

Hating to live in the city,
You moved your whole family into the blue-green haze.
Opening a path through pines for the moon to pass through;
Linking bamboo tubing to draw mountain stream water.
Worries now eased, not a white hair on your head;
Poetry, pure, face not all puffed up.
Of course no horses and carriages will come,
But still you close the gate that faces the cliff.

劉隱君山居　　　　　p. 14a

嫌在城中住；全家入翠微
開松通月過；接竹引泉歸
慮淡頭無白；詩清貌不肥
必無車馬至；猶掩向巖扉

47

30 | MY OFFICIAL RESIDENCE NEWLY COMPLETED

We made this residence right along the city wall;
First thought was to seek coolness in summer.
We sank a pool to take in all the streamlets,
Planted bamboo to cut off setting sunbeams.
The tenure is three years in all;
But I've not one thing rushing me.
I can't imagine what to report about,
Sitting peacefully, afraid I'll fail at this.

官舍初成   p. 14b

為宅傍城墙; 先求夏日凉
鑿池容衆水; 栽竹斷斜陽
官是三年滿; 身無一事忙
不知何補報; 安坐恐難當

31 | THE VERANDAH OF CLUSTERED SCENES

From this verandah, not only a single scene:
I'd describe them, but it's hard to name them all.
The Yangzi is near, and autumn shade comes early;
Mountains abound, so morning air is crisp.
Fragments of cloud moor in different trees;
Hungry cranes descend to the fields and search.
And then one assumes that when the deep night falls,
In the vast void will appear a brilliant moon.

會景軒   p. 14b

此中非一景; 欲狀固難名
江近秋陰早; 山多曉氣清
斷雲分樹泊; 饑鶴下田行
別擬深更至; 虛空看月明

32-33 | FOLLOWING THE RHYMES OF ZHU ZIFA, AND SENT AS A BRIEF EPISTLE TO MY FRIENDS AT GREEN DRAGON: TWO POEMS

I

South of my alley, north of my alley,
The ways to your houses aren't far.
But though it's my practice to sit in solitude,
I've troubled you gentlemen to visit now and then.
Gazing at the mountains, I resent the evening haze;
Listening to the rain, I imagine the springtime waves.
Let's just wait for a clear, sunlit day:
Then, come over, each carrying a jug of wine.

II

Who'd ever think I was living in the capital?
Can anyone deny the sheer purity of West Lake?
But my many illnesses prevent full joy in nature;
And poverty badly mitigates poetic sentiment.
I stick catkins in my hair to display spring feeling,
I take rubbings of old stelae to block out urban noise.
Along Pine River, how many leisured wanderers
Day and night get to hear the singing of the waves?

Due to the Jurchen occupation of northern China, the Southern Song Dynasty was compelled to move the capital to Hangzhou, renaming it *Lin'an*, "Temporary Refuge," reflecting their hope it would be so. The fifth line of the first poem may at first seem counterintuitive, as the mists hanging around mountains are always appreciated for their evocative beauty in both poetry and painting. But that very fact renders the line poignant, as now the poet wishes to gaze at the actual mountains with a clear line of vision! The unexpected resentment of the haze is quite consciously brought in. The point of the first two lines of the second poem is, that despite this now being the primary city of the dynasty, it sits on the banks of the beautiful and beloved West Lake, and so seems almost to be a country locale. The actual sound of tamping in taking rubbings may partially block outside noises, but also engaging in such an elegant practice helps distance the mind from worldly matters.

和朱子發韻兼簡青龍諸友二首　　pp. 14b–15a

(I)

巷南與巷北；相去路無多
以我常孤坐；勞君數見過
望山嫌夕靄；聽雨想春波
稍俟晴明日；相攜一醉過

(II)

雖說京華住；西湖豈不清
病多妨野興；貧甚損詩情
挿柳觀春意；粘碑隔市聲
松江幾聞客；日夕聽波鳴

34 | PEACH BLOSSOM TEMPLE

In ancient times, peach trees flourished here.
The temple has been named to honor them.
The stones are hidden, egrets perch on them;
The rapids, distant, heard by monks at night.
They scoop out well-water, yellow leaves and all,
Climb to the terrace, scattering white clouds.
Ge Hong! Goulou Magistrate refining Elixir!
There's no spot they don't meet you in this realm.

Ge Hong (Ko Hung 葛洪, 283–343), a founding father of Daoist alchemy, upon learning that a certain practitioner in Goulou had attained the Elixir, requested to be appointed magistrate here. This particular location is, of course, a Buddhist temple, but it may simply be so magical that Ge Hong appears to the monks. It is also possible that Ge Hong had a connection with it.

桃花寺　　　　　　　　p. 15a

舊有桃花樹; 人呼寺故名
石幽秋鷺上; 灘遠夜僧聞
汲井連黃葉; 登臺散白雲
燒丹勾漏令; 無處不逢君

35 | ON THE WAY TO THE TEMPLE OF GREAT COMPASSION

Green mosses cover the whole path;
Human traces get fewer as I go.
The little temple's evening bell rings vespers;
The deep woods let through only dim sunlight.
Spring is past, but wildflowers bloom all over;
Mountain birds fly homeward down the creek.
Sometimes I do meet with people:
Most returning from gathering magic herbs.

大慈道   p. 15b

青苔生滿路; 人迹至應稀
小寺鳴鐘晚; 深林透日微
野花春後發; 山鳥澗中飛
或有相逢者; 多因採藥歸

36 | Seeing off Pan Jingcan to Take Up Duties as Inspector in Lilu

The roads to Sichuan are as far as the sky:
Whole family with you, itinerary hard to figure out.
You're not going via the Three Gorges,
So you'll avoid the heartbreak of the gibbons' cries.
The garrison in a secret location, wildflowers few;
Cantilever roads deserted, singing with mountain rains.
Same-year graduates, same in desolation:
But on this trip *you* will make your name!

Here Zhao paints on a broader canvas than is usual for him. His
friend is undertaking a long excursion to Sichuan to take up an
important position at a military post. This conjures up the imagery
of the gibbons of the Three Gorges along the Yangzi River, whose
mournful cries are supposed to evoke heart-sickness in the
traveler; and the famed cantilever wood-plank roads built hugging
the cliffs of the towering mountains, a triumph of ancient Chinese
engineering, and often depicted in paintings set in this region.

送潘景參赴利路帳幹　　pp.15b–16a

蜀道如天遠；攜家難計程
不從三峽過；免聽幾猿聲
戍密野花少；棧虛山雨鳴
同年同寂寞；此去子成名

37 | AT THE WATER'S EDGE

At the water's edge I've moved now, late in life;
Steamy breezes fill the islets with green.
Duckweeds so thick it's impossible to fish;
Tall willow trees blocking the view of the stars.
Busy? That would be the monks passing by;
Leisurely? That would be listening to the rain.
I've thought about it, but have no long-range plan,
Only to stay here to the end, behind closed bramble gate.

水際   p. 16a

水際移居晚; 薰風綠滿汀
密萍妨下釣; 高柳礙觀星
忙是僧相過; 閒惟雨可聽
尋思非久計; 終憶自柴扃

38 | HOLDING THE RAILING

I force myself to get up, hold the railing, stand;
Fresh coldness suddenly invades.
The bells of temples all are sounding matins;
The shade of willows darkens half the pond.
I've been sick so long, but finally accept moxa;
Poverty so deep, I sometimes dream of gold.
Beside the lake, the weather's been delightful,
But I've dropped out of so many mountain hikes!

扶欄   p. 16a

強起扶欄立; 新寒陡見侵
鐘聲諸寺曉; 柳蔭半池陰
病久方憑艾; 貧深或夢金
湖邊好風日; 孤負幾登臨

39 | A Small Pavilion Dedicated to Old Man Ge

Tree-colors set off sparse lattices,
The whole a swath of simple purity.
A gentle breeze wafts down willow catkins;
The setting sun glows at bamboo tips.
This old man had nothing vulgar about him;
Even his two concubines filled with love of the Dao.
A wanderer, I come, and, attracted by plain walls,
Inscribe this poem, but leave out my name.

This poem describes a shrine to Ge Hong (see poem 34 and note).

葛翁小閣 p. 16b

樹色對疏櫺；橫陳一片清
微風楊葉下；斜日竹梢明
此老無塵事；雙姝亦道情
客來憐素壁；題句不題名

40 | Presented to the Bookseller Degree-Holder Chen Zongzhi

Surrounded on all four sides by books old and new,
All day long you sit right in the middle.
Your door faces the waters of the official canal;
Your eaves are shaded by green willow trees.
You always detain famous scholars to have a drink;
Often have you begged me to chant my poems!
But most of all, after fire torched all my books,
You've let me borrow yours for consultation.

This poem was written for a key figure in the cultural life of Zhao's day: bookseller, publisher and poet himself, Chen Qi (Ch'en Ch'i 陳起). Chen acted as patron to many contemporary poets, and was a champion of the Four Lings and others whom he termed the School of Rivers and Lakes, publishing a large anthology of their works, the *Rivers and Lakes Collection* (*Jianghu ji* 江湖集). Because a couplet included in the collection was declared by his enemies to be plagiarized, he was sent into exile and the woodblocks for printing the work were destroyed. Eventually he was able to return to Lin'an, his hometown, where his beloved book store was located.

贈賣書陳秀才宗之　　　pp. 16b–17a

四圍皆古今；永日坐中心
門對官河水；簷依柳樹陰
每留名士飲；屢索老夫吟
最感書燒盡；時容借檢尋

41 | DOCTOR FORBIDS CHESTNUTS

The night so long, not limited to one dream—
I'd write them down, but they're soon lost in haze.
I glance into the mirror: skin withered like dried jerky;
I comb my hair: some falls, looks just like frost.
If my aches and pains would ease off a bit,
I could think of ways to cure my poverty.
One thing I really love is chestnuts from the shore;
But this year, I don't dare to take a bite.

栗禁   p. 17a

宵長非一夢; 欲記已微茫
照鏡枯于腊; 梳頭落似霜
病痛如退愈; 貧窶又商量
所嗜惟崖栗; 今年不敢嘗

42 | A THOUSAND DAYS

Thousand-day tenure! Just passed half;
What karma leads me towards returning home?
This job of magistrate? Most things are easy;
And yet I'm never totally relaxed.
For planting magic herbs, I like the office garden;
Climbing city walls recalls home mountains.
My painstaking poems no one really likes,
So I just write them all over the doors and walls.

The standard tenure for official postings was three years, rounded out here to "a thousand days." The second and sixth lines indicate homesickness; Zhao looks forward to a period back home after the job is over.

千日   p. 17b

千日方過半; 何因便得還
就令凡事易; 不及一身閒
種术憐官地; 登城憶自山
苦吟無愛者; 寫在户庭間

58

43 | Presented to Zhang Yi

Since we last parted, not a single letter!
Now we meet again: both turned old!
The old mountains, streams, are far beyond war-beacons;
The months and years drag on as if in dream.
Your once-empty bag now holds a poetry manuscript;
Your unlined robe gives off the fragrance of wine.
We get to talking about that banquet at Rolling Stream,
We both recall how crazy we were back then.

贈張亦   p. 18a

一別無書信; 相逢各老蒼
山川烽外遠; 歲月夢中長
空橐成詩草; 單衣浣酒香
因言滾溪宴; 同憶舊時狂

44 | Paying a Visit to Han Zhongzhi, but He Was Not at Home–inscribed in his house on the stream

Your bamboo gate, deep in woods across the stream;
Your aging man guides me to search for you.
Although we never get to meet and talk,
At least I am able to view the woods and garden.
Wild vines at times impede my steps;
Mountain cicadas are chanting beautifully.
At the base of a cliff, a natural spring
Flows musically, in harmony with my heart.

訪韓仲止不遇題澗上　　　　p. 18b

隔澗竹扉深; 蒼童引客尋
雖然乖晤語; 猶自見園林
野蔓時妨步; 山蟬亦好吟
石根泉數斗; 清響應人心

45 | Tortoise Peak Temple

The stony path penetrates blue lotus;
 I came upon this place as if by chance.
The peak looms high, shot with autumn moonlight;
The cliff is split—rustic mist seeps through.
Fireflies, cold, cling to palm tree leaves;
A monk, at peace, meditates beside the well.
In this empty hall, I will stay overnight,
Just like sleeping up on Wild Goose Mountain.

龜峰寺　　　　p. 19a

石路入青蓮; 來遊出偶然
峰高秋月射; 巖裂野煙穿
螢冷粘櫻上; 僧閒坐井邊
虛堂留一宿; 宛似鴈山眠

46 | CAVE MASTER SHEN

On your desk, a scroll of talismans;
It must have been Black Mountain Mother who passed it on to you!
You spend whole days without saying a word;
You go whole years without eating a thing.
Clouds veil your brazier for refining Elixir;
Flowers float down the stream for washing herbs.
At times you hear the Mystic Tiger may emerge:
You go the cave entrance, where you perform a service.

沈洞主　　　　　　　p. 19b

案上陰符卷; 應逢驪母傳
無言過永日; 不食度終年
雲覆燒丹竈; 花浮洗藥泉
時聞有玄虎; 來禮洞門前

47 | FOLLOWING THE RHYMES OF A POEM FROM COUNTY COMMANDER PAO

You entertain monks in your autumn pavilion,
Yourself as peaceful as the monks.
You wash your teeth at the cold mountain stream,
Burn incense as you face the distant hills.
Wild birds steal fruit from your trees;
Your boy returns from borrowing sutras.
If anything further should strike your interest,
You compose poems, then inscribe them all over your house.

和鮑縣尉   pp. 19b–20a

留僧秋閣上；身自伴僧閒
漱齒臨寒水；焚香對遠山
野禽偷果去；童子借經還
餘興成詩句；高題屋柱間

48 | HAPPY THAT XU DAOHUI COMES BY TO VISIT

Drinking only tea, you've grown even thinner;
I'm starting to wonder if you're becoming an Immortal!
Recently you've written few poems;
But at leisure, you'll do paintings and pass them on.
You crossed River Xiao in wind and snow;
Inscribed your name on cliffs of sacred Mount Heng.
But you kept up with any news that was about:
Every morning, questioning travelers' boats.

Addressed to Xu Zhao, line 4 is a rare piece of evidence that any
of the Four Lings might have painted.

喜徐道暉至   pp. 20a–b

嗜茶身益瘦；兼恐欲通仙
近作詩全少；聞成畫亦傳
瀟江風雪渡；嶽石姓名鐫
自接來消息；朝朝問客船

49 | A LITTLE BOAT

My little boat! It takes me everywhere!
It brings me closer to nature, day by day.
Though blocked by wild plants like lotus leaves,
The light-foot gulls are like Immortals, free.
So calm, I think: The water in this lake,
How much city dust has it washed away?
I'd love to build a fisherman's hut right here,
But my karma for this sort of thing is void.

小舟   p. 20b

小舟隨處去；幽意日相親
野草妨荷葉；輕鷗似逸人
閒思此湖水；曾洗幾京塵
甚欲營漁屋；空虛未有因

50 | AT THE TOMB OF LIN BU

Plum blossom trees, a thousand blooming white;
Yet this is not the village of old times.
I pour out some of the wine I bought and brought,
Libation for your soul, become immortal.
The short stele leans over, caught by vines;
The empty mound is overgrown with bamboo.
But still return the cranes to pay a call:
Once purified, I wish I could talk with them.

Lin Bu (Lin Pu 林逋, 968–1028) was a major poet of the early
Song, best known for his hermit-like residence at West Lake
when the nearby city was more like a village. He had "plum
blossom trees as his wives, and cranes as his children." Lin was
buried at his beloved West Lake.

林逋墓下   p. 20b

梅花千樹白; 不是舊時村
傾我酤來酒; 酹君仙去魂
短碑藤倚蔓; 空塚竹行根
猶有歸來鶴; 清時欲與論

51 | FOR A MONK AT FIVE PEAKS

Your peak is shaped like the palm of a hand,
    wrapped round in blue-green;
Monk of white hair, you guide this guest
    to view the entire scene.
As fallen leaves all decompose,
    the muddy path turns slippery;
When setting sunlight falls away,
    the stone bridge becomes cold.
A waterfall sounds very near—
    much farther than I thought!
I reckoned calamus easy to find,
    but gathering some is hard.
Please let me take one of these peaks
    so I could live on it;
I'd willingly quit my official post
    to gather here with you.

Although Zhao, like the other Lings, favored five-character per line
regulated verse, he and the others also wrote in seven-character
meter, as here. The calamus mentioned in line 11 was one of
those herbs considered capable of extending longevity, if properly
prepared and taken.

示五峰僧   p. 21a

峯形如掌翠相環；頭白山僧引客看
積葉壞來泥徑滑；斜陽移去石橋寒
近聞瀑布尋還遠；易得菖蒲采極難
分我一峯於此住；與師相聚願辭官

52 | SEEING OFF MONK SHI ON A FUND-RAISING EXPEDITION

Braving the cold, where are you going,
    all alone like this?
"To build a cloister here on Soul Mountain,
    something we can't afford."
Bring your poetry manuscript
    to show potential donors;
Your herb-stove you leave in the care
    of other resident monks.
In setting sunlight along the shore
    you'll walk past withered leaves;
Passing waterfalls from stone cliffs,
    you'll hear sounds of cracking ice.
I know you will succeed,
    your karma causing great response:
And when you return, gold and azure
    will thrust through layered clouds.

When new buildings or refurbishing of old ones was necessary, monks would embark on excursions to raise funds from donors, who would "gain merit" by giving. See poems 90 and 152 on the subject.

送奭上人抄化　　　pp. 21b–22a

冒寒獨向何方去；為建靈山閣未能
詩卷帶呈看疏客；藥爐留借共房僧
夕陽岸上行枯葉；瀑布巖前聽拆冰
事到有緣隨處應；回來金碧入雲層

53 | HAVING MOVED, I WOULD BE GRATEFUL FOR VISITS FROM FRIENDS

I've rented a house for regular folks,
    and it too is quite pure:
Here I lodge my ailing body,
    floating around too long.
Bamboo shoots emerge between cracks in bricks,
    path-tiles on the ground;
The mountains, viewed above neighbor's trees,
    thrust upwards, all in green.
There is a well, the water sweet,
    just right for brewing tea;
I have no flowers, though, to plant:
    I'll do with empty vases.
South of my alley, north of my alley
    few acquaintances:
I'd be deeply moved, my poets,
    if from far you'd knock on my gate!

移居謝友人見過　　　　　pp. 23a–b

賃得民居亦自清; 病身於此寄飄零
笋從壞砌磚中出; 山在鄰家樹上青
有井極甘便試茗; 無花可插任空瓶
巷南巷北相知少; 感爾詩人遠扣扃

54 | AGAIN JOURNEYING TO NORTH MOUNTAIN, FOLLOWING THE DESIGNATED RHYMES

Now strolling, now meditating
    in the pavilion beside the stream:
Everywhere, spring breezes,
    every door unlocked.
Flying catkins accompany me
    white like my withering hairs;
Distant mountains imitate me,
    robed in blue hermit's robes.
Far, far away I wander,
    deeper into hazy mist;
It seems I've passed this way before,
    in one of my dreams.
I think I must have been Hermit Lin
    in a former life:
Late in life, not drinking any more,
    finally sobered up.

The title refers to the "rhyme words," characters distributed by the host of a literary gathering as part of a poetry game. Participants were required to use the assigned characters as part of the rhyming scheme of verses they then extemporaneously produced. The personification of the mountains in line 4 is unusual in Chinese poetry. Hermit Lin is probably Lin Bu, see poem 50 and note.

再遊北山和韻　　　　pp. 23b–24a

或行或坐水邊亭; 處處春風户不扃
飛絮伴人衰鬢白; 遠山學我道衣青
迢遙更入烟霏去; 髣髴如曾夢寐經
恐是前生林處士; 晚年不飲至今醒

55 | AN EVENING VIEW FROM THE TOWER OF MANY SCENES

Setting sun, the balustrade
    as high as the wild geese;
Strolling about, I feel my youthful spirit
    has returned.
The tide is rising along the ocean shore,
    faint white in the distance;
The wheat is flourishing south of the Huai,
    winding in miles of green.
Merchants from afar moor their ships
    in pursuit of local profit;
An old monk points at a jar
    to explain the shape of the county.
A dying wind suddenly carries
    bugle calls from a camp:
The sound leads to worries about the frontier . . .
    I can't bear hearing it.

Couplet 6 is a good example of the original and sometimes unique imagery from everyday life in the poetry of the Four Lings.

多景樓晚望　　　　　pp, 24a–b

落日欄干與鴈平; 往來疑有舊英靈
潮生海口微茫白; 麥秀淮南迤邐青
遠賈泊舟趨地利; 老僧指甕說州形
殘風忽送吹營角; 聲引邊愁不可聽

56 | Rising from my Sickbed

My body like a skinny crane,
    soon down to skin and bones;
Doing nothing but lying in bed
    already ten days or more.
A morning visitor has heard of me,
    and brings me herbs to take;
A rustic monk, to care for me,
    sneaks out to bring me sutras.
My strength so low I feel as if
    my clothes weigh heavily;
My talent, gone, impossible to invite
    the muse of inkstone, brush.
There's only my heartfelt love of flowers
    that hasn't died away:
I gather chrysanthemums wherever they are,
    to put in my empty vases.

病起   pp. 24b–25a

身如瘦鶴已伶俜; 一臥兼旬更有零
朝客偶知親送藥; 野僧相保密持經
力微尚覺衣裳重; 才退難邀筆硯靈
惟有愛花心未已; 遍分黃菊插空瓶

57 | A POETIC EPISTLE TO EDITOR SUN

In my empty study, like a clod,
    hard passing the time of day;
How much the more, now middle-aged
    and sleep's just not enough.
I wash a cauldron, boil vegetables
    to serve to my few guests;
Roll up the blinds—the man is hoeing,
    transplanting chrysanthemums.
My autumn clothes, because of illness,
    now changed to monks' cassocks;
My temple hairs each chilly morning—
    half fall from the comb.
My grateful thanks to well-placed friends
    with office libraries:
Allowing me at will to borrow
    any books I want.

簡孫正字

p. 25a

空齋兀兀難消日；況入中年睡亦疎
洗釜煮蔬留客飯；卷簾移菊看人鋤
秋衣因病全更衲；曉鬢迎寒半脫梳
多謝貴交芸閣裏；許令隨意借官書

58 | BORROWING A RESIDENCE ON THE LAKE SHORE

I've left my job, and come back home,
    as poor as I was before!
I've borrowed this garden, which happens to be
    right near Painted Bridge.
The panoramic view requires
    no wine in the spring;
Pure meditation need not prevent
    reading books at night.
The harbor's tiny, only taking
    boats of men of leisure;
The trees hang low, blocking access
    to friends who come in carriages.
Previously, in cities,
    I accumulated dusty karma;
Long have I wished to live by the lake
    for a year or so at least.

借居湖上　　　　　　　　pp. 25a–b

出仕歸來貧似舊；借園偶近畫橋居
縱觀不用春攜酒；清坐何妨夜讀書
港小只通閒客棹；樹低多礙故人車
向時城裏緣塵土；久欲湖邊住歲餘

72

59 | SENDING AN ANCIENT JAR TO A FRIEND

This little jar is simple, pure,
    no ornaments at all;
It proves to be from Yin–Shang times,
    passed down to the present.
One spot is damaged—I fear some vulgar hand
    just grabbed it there;
When it was cast, an auspicious star
    must have shined on it.
For ages, hidden deep in earth,
    no bell-tone could ring out;
Now it holds a little water,
    deepening blue-green patina.
This I present, Oh noble one!
    to you to place on your desk,
Thus culling antique feeling for
    the new poems you will write!

Zhao is sending his friend a truly precious object as a gift, a plain cast-bronze "jar" (*hu* 壺) from the Yin or Shang (1766–1154 BCE), the earliest archaeologically confirmed Chinese dynasties. The unornamented nature of this particular example would especially embody the aesthetic of simplicity called *pingdan* (平淡, literally "even and bland"). This is the literati aesthetic par excellence, implying rich profundity, and applicable to poetry, painting, calligraphy, other works of art, and even to human character.

送古壺與人　　　　　　p. 25b

小壺純素無文采；驗是殷商物至今
損處怕教凡手觸；鑄時應有吉星臨
久藏厚土金聲盡；微貯清泉翠色深
持贈高人安几席；為勾古意入新吟

60 | [Sent to] Deng Hanching

All alone, just one man,
    my life has never been stable;
Nor have I any books at all
    to follow me around.
Hurried, I passed through the world of men
    then came to days of leisure;
Aging, I met with the Court's employ
    for just a little time.
Encountering snow, I tell myself,
    "The roads of life are bitter!"
Viewing pines, I grieve at length
    I've delayed "buying my mountain."
Withering, withering, whitening hairs
    in cold lamplight now:
I've finished writing this little poem:
    to whom do you think I'll send it?

Here Zhao clearly laments his failed career, having received only
a minor and brief government appointment late in life. Thus there
was no possibility of acquiring the resources needed for "buying
my mountain" or the libraries and boats (see 61) enjoyed by the
wealthy. See also 63.

鄧漢卿　　　　　pp. 25b–26a

單獨一身長不定; 亦無書卷得相隨
忙過人世當閒日; 老遇朝廷用少時
衝雪自言行路苦; 看松長恨買山遲
蕭蕭白髮寒燈下; 寫就詩篇欲寄誰

74

61 | COLD-FOOD FESTIVAL AT SOLITARY MOUNT

In the third month, fragrant flora
    all along the lakeshore;
Travelers here, worries gone,
    stroll wherever they please.
Clear sky, butterflies' spread wings
    now dotted evenly with powder;
Rain presses the willow catkins,
    not broidery as yet.
Lines come to me—I inscribe them
    on walls of leisure places;
I have no money, hard to rent
    boats used by the rich.
Most I love this place where the Recluse
    slept in noble style:
Every day here, spring breezes
    are music of strings and winds.

Solitary Mount was the place of reclusion at West Lake of the
hermit-poet Lin Bu, the "Recluse" (see poem 50 and note).

孤山寒食   p. 26a

三月芳菲在水邊; 旅人消困亦隨緣
晴舒蝶翅初勻粉; 雨壓楊花未放綿
有句自題閒處壁; 無錢難買貴時船
最憐隱者高眠地; 日日春風是筦絃

62 | SENT TO HONORABLE MASTER WEN AT MAO MOUNTAIN

How many times have I written poems
    and sent them to your mountain?
I wonder where you get the books
    that you read all the time?
On lichen-mottled rocks in fall
    you chant painstaking poems;
On the Dais of the Constellations,
    at night you worship, cold.
You've renamed your pet crane—
    you call him, he doesn't come!
You come upon broken stelae—
    inscriptions tough for rubbings.
I always think of you, and always
    want to seek you out:
The magic herbs you grow and prepare
    I'd certainly imbibe.

The Master addressed would be a Daoist practitioner at Mao Mountain, one of the key sacred mountains of religious or alchemical Daoism.

寄茅山溫尊師   p. 26b

幾度題詩寄入山; 不知何處得書看
莓苔石上秋吟苦; 星斗壇中夜拜寒
鶴改新名呼未至; 碑逢斷刻打應難
憶師每欲尋師去; 芝朮栽成自可湌

63 | AFTER AN ILLNESS IN THE CAPITAL

Long time spent in the capital,
    depleting my Mind of Dao;
Who of my friends participates
    in this rise-and-fall?
Lying in my Spring tower sickbed,
    swallows my only companions;
Inscribing poems in West Lake temples,
    monks chanting them for me.
Three months now I've not received
    a letter from family;
One strand of white has newly invaded
    the black of temple-hair.
I've long since known this is not the time
    for "Admonitions Against Hunting";
All that's left—up in the mountains,
    to refine the Gold Elixir.

The poem is another (see 60) evocative depiction of the poet's
disappointment in his aborted official career. He understands that
he will never rise to the level of a Censor, an official tasked with
submitting "Admonitions" to the Emperor, cautioning against such
extravagances as elaborate, costly Imperial hunts.

京華病後　　　　　　　　　p. 27a

久在京華損道心; 故人誰與念升沈
春樓臥病燕相伴; 湖寺題詩僧為吟
三月不逢家信至; 一莖新有鬢絲侵
早知諫獵非時節; 只有山中自養金

64 | Passing Through Yiyang

In three months, three times
    have I trudged through Yiyang;
The suffering of this life of mine
    is beyond comprehension.
How many years for the rapids' waves
    to grind those rocks all smooth?
Just last night's frost was all it took
    to redden all river maples.
I've already reckoned I must be on the road
    through the Winter Solstice;
It's pitiful! These wayside inns
    are not the home I crave.
To sleep in noble style I long have vowed
    to go up to the mountains;
All I lack is the Daoists' method,
    there in the blue-green coils.

過弋陽

p. 27b

三月三番過弋陽；吾生辛苦莫思量
磨圓灘石幾年浪；丹盡江楓昨夜霜
已算中途當度臘；更憐抵舍未為鄉
高眠舊有山中約；只欠青螺道士方

65 | SEVERAL DAYS

For several days, the autumn wind
    has cheated this sick man:
It's blown down all the yellow leaves,
    into the courtyard weeds.
The woods once sparse, they would allow
    far mountains to appear,
When—no! Again they're half concealed
    as clouds come drifting through.

A delightful quatrain very much in the manner of Yang Wanli
(see Introduction, p 12), in which the last line springs a Zen-like
surprise, in this case, a revelation of just how nasty the autumn
wind is being to the poor sick poet, preventing him one way or
the other from viewing properly the beautiful mountains in the
distance.

數日　　　　　　　　p. 28a

數日秋風欺病夫；盡吹黃葉下庭蕪
林疎放得遙山出；又被雲遮一半無

66 | AT NIGHT RETURNING TO JADE
PURITY SHRINE

Before the cliff, the cassia blossoms
    haven't opened yet;
I've come to seek out in this shrine
    the Daoist Master here.
As light rain falls, the pine tree road
    turns completely dark . . .
But—fireflies suddenly come flying out,
    illumining blue-green lichens.

玉清夜歸　　　　　　　p. 28a

巖前未有桂花開；觀裏閒尋道士來
微雨過時松路黑；野螢飛出照青苔

79

67 | INSCRIBED IN THE POETRY SCROLL OF DAOIST [?] AT THE SHRINE OF FOUR SAGES

The entire shrine surrounded by peach blossoms
    like embroidery;
Willow trees down two embankments
    are greener than the clouds!
This traveler will only wander
    in daylight with clear skies;
The misty rain here, morning and night—
    it all belongs to you!

In the original edition of Zhao's works, an hiatus is indicated before "Daoist," and this would have been his name. In later anthologies, the hiatus is suppressed. The tone is tongue-in-cheek throughout. Zhao plays the role of the sort of obtuse tourist who insists on perfect weather before going forth, whereas the Daoist-poet shows in his poems that he is aware of the great beauty of nature in all seasons and all weathers. The statement in line 2 is nearly surreal in effect, anticipating by many centuries such effects as synaesthesia and surrealism in modern poetry.

題四聖觀[闕]道士詩卷　　　p. 28b

一觀桃花紅似錦; 兩堤楊柳綠於雲
遊人只是遊晴晝; 煙雨朝昏盡屬君

68 | WHITE ROCK CLIFF

Who burns fine incense,
  and worships Li Shaohe?
Faint sounds of bells and chimes
  I hear now in my dream . . .
I rise from bed, and using
  a sleeve of my layman's robe
Wrap up a swath of cloud
  that's floating past the railing.

Li Shaohe (Li Shao-ho 李少和) was a native of Yongjia who lived at this place as a Daoist practitioner. Although general opinion considered it to be a spot haunted by demons, Li was perceptive enough to recognize its auspicious character. The poet considers even the clouds scudding by to be sacred.

白石巖   p. 28b

誰炷清香禮少君; 數聲金磬夢中聞
起來閒把青衣袖; 裹得闌干一片雲

69 | HAVING INVITED A GUEST

At the season of Ripe Plums,
    it rains on every house;
At the pond of green reeds,
    everywhere the croaking of the frogs.
We had a date, he hasn't come,
    and it's past midnight now:
By myself, I click chess pieces
    in the light of a guttering lamp.

This is probably the most anthologized poem by Zhao. Two lines
from it were carved in a pair of fine seals in by the great Qi Baishi
(Ch'i Pai-shih 齊白石, 1864–1957) nearly seven centuries later.

約客   p. 28b

黃梅時節家家雨; 青草池塘處處蛙

有約不來過夜半; 閒敲棋子落燈花

Seal carving is as highly prized as painting and calligraphy among the literati arts of China, although it has yet to be fully recognized in the West. These two seals (reproduced in vermilion on the cover) were carved by the master painter, calligrapher, and seal carver, Qi Baishi, one of the greatest traditional Chinese artists of the modern era. One of the seals is based on the second line, and one on the fourth line of Zhao's poem 69. In the first seal, Qi has used a picture of a frog to stand for that last word in the second line. The seal dates from 1935.

In the second seal, Qi has combined text to the left with a "still-life" to the right. On a table are laid out a playing board for *weiqi* ("surround chess," known as *go* in Japan), with several pieces to the side, a pot of tea with two cups, and an oil lamp, burning. The text, in Qi's signature seal calligraphy—powerful, neo-archaic, almost primeval in impact—is the single seven-word last line from this quatrain by Zhao Shixiu. Thus we have a modern artist reaching back to the twelfth century for his poetic inspiration, as if it were only yesterday.

70 | On an Autumn Day Traveling to the Hermitage Perched in Mist

On impulse, I enter the isolated village;
My soul comes to life among autumn waters.
Chrysanthemums are opened, but the path is so narrow!
The lotuses are done, so the pond seems wider now.
Pine shadows darken the hut, cliff-suspended;
A temple bell sounds, from somewhere in the mountain.
Such a wondrous excursion cannot tire me:
Dawn sunlight illumines the pass through the pines.

秋日遊栖霞菴　　　　　pp. 29b–30a

乘興入孤村; 神凝秋水間
菊開嫌徑小; 荷盡覺池寬
林影懸崖屋; 鐘聲何處山
清遊殊未倦; 初日照松關

71 | THE WOMAN YI ZHEN

Abruptly, she was able not to eat;
Drinking only water, she passed her middle years.
I know such a thing is hard to fake:
She makes one believe there are really Immortals!
Her body and face showed no sign of blood-color;
Her robes gave off a perfumed mist.
I hear the road to Jasper Pond
Appeared quite clearly right before her eyes.

This remarkable woman, whose name means "Unified Truth," was
a Daoist nun said to have achieved immortality. Such practitioners
were believed capable of living without eating. In her case, she
apparently was shown the way to Jasper Pond in the far west, the
residence of the Queen Mother of the West (西王母), chief of all
female Immortals.

一真姑 　　　　　　　　p. 30a

忽然能不食；飲水度中年
此事知難偽；令人信有仙
形容無血色；衣袂有香煙
聽說瑤池路；分明在目前

72 | SPENDING IN THE NIGHT IN MY BOAT, MOORED IN A RIVER INLET, I HEAR THAT YUAN THE EIGHTH HAS BEEN ASSIGNED TO AN OFFICIAL POSITION AT THIS PLACE

You journeyed to the Cinnabar Halls—
    already, three promotions!
I've just floated along the waves,
    now two years have passed.
Sword suspended, at dawn you've rushed
    to the Phoenix-Pair Towers;
While I, on misty ripples spend the night
    in a single fishing boat.
You've entertained your parents always
    amongst the Blue Clouds,
Though my home village I've left behind,
    to live beneath the sky.
If I report my life to you,
    you'll surely laugh at me:
A small thatched hut, planting yams
    in the fields, slashed-and-burned.

Mr. Yuan is eighth-eldest in his cohort of brothers and male cousins. This humorous poem compares the poet's life line-by-line with that of a friend who has succeeded in the world of officialdom. Cinnabar Halls, Phoenix-Pair Towers, and Blue Clouds all refer to the Imperial palace. Ironically, both men are in the same locale for the night, one serving in his current post as local magistrate, the poet spending the night in his little boat.

夜宿江浦聞元八改官寄此　　　p. 30b

君遊丹陛已三遷; 我泛滄浪亦二年
劍佩曉趨雙鳳闕; 烟波夜宿一漁船
交親盡在青雲上; 鄉曲都拋白日邊
若報生涯應笑殺; 結茅栽芋種畬田

"Renouncing the Official Seal" from the hand scroll *Scenes from the Life of Tao Yuanming* by Chen Hongshou (Ch'en Hung-shou 陳洪綬, 1598–1652), dated 1650, ink and color on silk, Honolulu Museum of Art accession 1912.1. Although all four Lings make some mention of Tao Yuanming's life (see poems 10, 81, 197, 201 and their notes), Weng Juan In poem 78 make extensive reference to a particular poem by Tao.

62 POEMS BY WENG JUAN

(Lingshu 靈舒, d. after 1214)

Page numbers refer to the one-chapter collected works of Weng Juan, "Collection from the West Cliff" (*Xiyan ji* 西巖集) in the *Siku quanshu*. These translations were previously published as *West Cliff Poems: The Poetry of Weng Chüan* (Tokyo and Toronto: ahadada books, 2010).

73 | Echoing the Poem by Edict Attendant Chen, "A Banquet Gathering in a Lakeside Pavilion on an Autumn Day"

In just one evening, a singing rain comes in
And changes autumn's visage overnight.
Lake and mountains then begin to clear:
Breeze-blown mists bring on a subtle chill.
The Attendant has set out a festive spread,
Opening this pavilion to enjoy the fresh scene.
He thinks of us who dwell in these same forests,
Inviting us to share the view with him.
Emerald reeds spread over the near shore,
White clouds cap the distant peaks.
Vaguely sensed—an orchid bridge, so fragrant;
In imagination—the purity of Rivers Xiao and Xiang.
Touching transformation, our poems are quickly finished;
Worries about success entirely put aside.
Given such "excursions with the Creative Power,"
What need for realms of gods or of Immortals?

It should be noted that another of the Four Lings, Zhao Shixiu, has a poem with two alternate titles: *Edict Attendant Chen's Lakeside Pavilion* (陳待制湖樓), or *Chen Shuiyun's Pavilion for Excursions with the Creative Power* (陳水雲與造物遊之樓). Fang Hui (Fang Ho 1227–1305), who anthologized the poem in his influential work, *The Essence of Regulated Verse from the Literary Constellation of Paradise* (*Yingkui lüsui* 瀛奎律髓), comments that a pavilion of this name is located near the city of Yongjia, and is two stories high. Thus the penultimate line in Weng's poem may have been intended as a reference to the pavilion's name.

和陳待制秋日湖樓宴集篇　　　　p. 2a

一夕鳴雨來；秋容變俄頃
湖山屬初霽；風煙帶微冷
侍臣設芳筵；開樓玩澄景
懷我林下人；招攜共觀省
碧草鋪近洲；白雲冒遙嶺
依稀蘭杠香；髣髴瀟湘淨
撫化篇忽成；達生累全屏
即是造物遊；何必神仙境

74 | GATHERING HERBS IN THE MOUNTAINS

The cliffsides grow the magic herbs;
And usually, few are those who come.
But now I gather as many as I like,
Climbing high, so tired I forget returning.
Enriching the leaves, the dew that moistens them;
Deep roots imbibing the flesh of the earth.
Lovely light beautifies my hermit's satchel;
Fragrant vapors fill my rippling robe.
I wash the herbs with pure stream water,
Dry them in the brilliance of the sun.
Preparing them, I follow prescribed methods,
Then eat them to absorb their benefits.
Healing ailments, nurturing Heavenly harmony:
Could Immortals' prescriptions ever fail me?
Participating in the way of ancient cultivation,
Thus I'll put off the time of my decay.
And if my time of decay can be put off,
Why should I hustle about the ten-thousand affairs?

Throughout the history of Chinese thought, there has been an interesting tension between acceptance and rejection of the idea that through the preparation of elixirs, including the use of special herbs to be found in the mountains, longevity and even immortality might be achieved. Weng's first poem (73) draws an explicit contrast between the "Creative Power" of nature, and the putatively imaginative realm of gods and immortals, while this one finds him actively engaged in the quest for longevity achieved through imbibing specially prepared magical herbs.

山中採藥　　　　　　pp. 4a–b

嚴崖產靈藥; 等閒人顧稀
採掇獲所願; 躋登倦忘歸
沃葉帶露滋; 深根涵土肌
妍光媚幽筬; 芳氣盈我衣
濯以清澗泉; 曝之太陽暉
製治擬如法; 服食從所宜
除痾養天和; 仙方豈吾欺
協彼古修意; 庶用延將衰
將衰儻得延; 萬事焉足為

75 | POEM ON WANDERING OFF AS AN IMMORTAL

The dawn sun climbs to the great void,
Flowing beams touching budding sprouts.
Alongside, pentacolored clouds,
Scintillating, full of energy.
What I want is to eat them up,
And rise in my body far through distant mists.
May I be decked in sash-ornaments of purity,
May I be outfitted with a floating chariot!
Even Three Magic Mountains are not enough for me!
A thousand years of age? Who says that is too much!
"Enlightenment!"—Those people slaving away,
They're no different from flowers that last a single spring.

In the final couplet the poet is poking fun at certain Buddhists.

游仙篇   p. 1a

旭日升太虛; 流光到萌芽
旁有五雲氣; 煥爛含精華
所願服食之; 躋身眇長霞
帶我清泠佩; 飛我欻忽車
三山不足期; 千齡詎云賒
悟彼勞生人; 無異芳春花

76 | POEM ON TREADING EMPTINESS

The Mystic Root spreads magical leaves:
This wondrous transformation, not for ordinary men.
Let me join with the pure Yang energy,
And elevate my soul up through the void!
Let me refine Elixir, obtain longevity,
And join the ranks of the assembled Immortals!
I'll ascend, a guest at the Jade Emperor's court,
Waited on by serving girls—the stars!
Far below, the realm all full of dust:
Why make that putrescence my neighbor?

步虛辭　　　　　　　pp. 1a-b

玄根布靈葉; 妙化無常人
結茲清陽氣; 挺我空洞神
煉度得長生;列籍齊眾真
登賓玉皇家; 執侍羅星嬪
茫茫塵中區; 荒穢何足鄰

77 | THE ANCIENT WAY

The ancient Way today is seen no more.
Relations now have not the ancient depth.
It is so hard, so hard to form a friendship,
Hard to see a pair of eyes that shine!
The green pine grows upon the mount of green:
Steadfastness, loyalty beyond compare.
Transplant it right beside the marketplace
And vulgar men will hold it in contempt.
The distant Way—quite easy to pursue?
Once out the gate—regrets start to be felt!
Sir, see those clouds, up there in the sky:
What further need to hustle and compete?
Do not say poverty lacks any ease:
Find ease in poverty, earn solid fame.

古道　　　　　　　　　pp. 4a-b

古道今不見;今交非古情
交情亦何難;難逢雙目明
青松生青山;貞節莫與并
植之厘郭旁;流俗多所輕
遠道豈易行;出門悔吝生
君看天上雲;何心更營營
勿言貧未安;安貧存令名

78 | INSCRIBED ON LIN SUIZHI'S "PAVILION OF TRUE MEANING"

You've built a pavilion to breathe in the vast void,
Towering high, beside the Southern Mountains.
The Southern Mountains have a wondrous feeling,
White clouds ever floating slowly by.
Flourishing flowers glitter on your autumn hedges,
Hidden fragrance coming forth in greeting.
Thick brew in hand, you face them, and you drink,
Transcending the worries that consumed your soul.
Supreme happiness!—Why seek it somewhere external?
Marvelous images, hard to capture in words!
So expansively, you've gotten Jingjie's spirit:
A thousand years later, you're able to grasp it well.

The whole poem is made up of allusions to a famous poem, number five in the series *Drinking Wine*, by Tao Qian (T'ao Ch'ien 陶謙, 365-427), also known as Yuanming and Jingjie. In that poem, Tao speaks of building a place of reclusion away from the troubled world, where chrysanthemums, his favorite flowers, grow, and the Southern Mountains can be glimpsed in the distance, with their implication of longevity. "In all these things, there lies a True Meaning / I'd speak of it, but have already lost the words," wrote Tao, echoing in turn a passage in the writings of Daoist philosopher Zhuangzi (fourth century BC), who said that a fish trap exists to capture fish; when the fish are captured, one discards the trap. And words exist to capture meaning; when one has captured the meaning, one discards or forgets the words.

題林遂之真意亭   p. 4b

結亭納虛豁；崔嵬進南山
南山有佳致；白雲多往還
繁英燦秋籬；幽芳復相闋
濁醪對之飲；超此神慮閒
至樂豈外求；妙象難言間
曠哉靖節風；千載君能攀

79 | On a Winter's Day Climbing to the Pavilion of Rich Views

I've never embarked on the ocean's changing waters:
Why have my comings and goings lacked stability?
Now a light mist splits off from the nearby suburbs,
And snow piled high caps the distant peaks.
Fishing boats float beyond geese on the spit;
Monks' quarters appear among trees on the island.
In this evening cold, it's hard to stand alone:
Done chanting my little poem, I return.

冬日登富覽亭　　　　pp. 6–b

未委海潮水；往來何不閒

輕烟分近郭；積雪盍遥山

漁舸汀鴻外；僧廊島樹間

晚寒難獨立；吟竟小詩還

80 | Sent to the Alchemist Li of Nine-Flowers Mountain

You've traveled throughout the southeastern districts,
And even been to see the Yangzi River's source.
In sleeve-pockets, you carry Goulou Mountain herbs;
And you are a descendent of Laozi himself!
You're off to live among the clouds that are like you,
"Withering and flourishing" you won't discuss at all.
The peaks of Nine-Flowers are the greenest that exist:
Facing the gate of your old residence there.

See Zhao Shixiu (34) for alchemy and the Goulou Mountains.

贈九華李丹士　　　　p. 6b

行徧東南地；曾看江水源

袖藏勾漏藥；身是老君孫

去住雲相似；枯榮事不論

九華峯最碧；相對舊柴門

81 | LIVING IN RECLUSION

My bramble gate I close, then open up:
Living in reclusion, called a "no-talent" man.
Transplanting pines, roots drip mountain earth;
Purchasing rocks, covered with stream moss.
I imbibe herbs trusted for becoming immortal;
I never *had* a job that I could quit.
So why write a poem called *Retiring Back Home?*

The last line refers to a famous poem by Tao Qian (see illustration p. 88) on the occasion of his quitting his job as magistrate of Pengze. This poem by Weng Juan, with minor variations and a different title ("My Hut"), is also attributed to another of the Four Lings, Xu Ji, by Yoshikawa Kōjirō in *An Introduction to Sung Poetry*, translated by Burton Watson (Harvard University Press, 1967), p. 173. Such confusions of authorship were common in certain periods of Chinese poetry; in this case, it is an indication of the stylistic closeness of all of the Four Lings. For the Chinese text of the Xu Ji version, see Xu Ji, *Erhwei t'ing shiji* 二薇亭詩集 (ed. of the *Siku chuanshu*), p. 23b. It is here included under the heading, *buyi* 補遺, "addenda of omitted items" (also in the addenda to Xu's collection in the *Sungshi chao*, whose editors may first have made this double attribution), implying that the Weng Juan attribution may be somewhat more reliable, as the poem is included in the regular section of Weng's collected works.

幽居   pp. 6b–7a

蓬户掩還開； 幽居稱不才
移松連嶠土； 買石帶溪苔
藥信仙方服； 衣從古樣裁
本無官可棄； 何用賦歸來

82 | On a Spring Day, Echoing a Poem by Liu Mingyuan

No matter, the sound of raindrops from the eaves:
The wind has brought back last night's clear skies.
The stairs are covered with the green of spring plants,
And a few petals fallen lightly from blossoms.
Know your lot in life, and poverty can be enjoyed;
Stop competing—even your dreams will be serene.
I observe how you discuss the recluse life:
Like me, you wish to escape from fame.

春日和劉明遠　　　　　　　　p. 7a

不奈滴簷聲;風回昨夜晴
一堦春草碧;幾片落花輕
知分貧堪樂;無營夢亦清
看君話幽隱;如我願逃名

83 | Presented to Ge Tianmin

Long ago, Monk Yanben lived like this,
And his pure name has been handed down for ages.
Would fine "bagged rice" ever come your way?
Yourself, you gather kindling for your fires.
Willow shadows join your mountain pavilion;
Lake-ripples invade your bamboo hedge.
Morning, evening, nothing else you want
Except to spend your time chanting new poems.

Monk Yanben was the great Tang poet Jia Dao, who actually withdrew from monastic life to become a degree-holding scholar. As noted, his poetry was a particular inspiration for the Four Lings (see Introduction, p. 16, and poem 21).

贈葛天民　　　　　　　　p. 7a

燕本昔如此; 清名千載垂
誰將囊米施; 自拾束薪炊
栁影連山閣; 湖波浸竹籬
朝昏無別事; 只是欲吟詩

84 | THE OLD PLUM BLOSSOM TREE AT THE CLOISTER OF MONK DAO

Solitary, towering, not touched by specks of dust,
Ancient, strange—who planted it long ago?
Its immortal soul rode off upon a sky-raft;
Its dragon body returned, covered with snow.
Branches coldly reflected in the water;
A single spot of moss mottling the bark.
And the crazy poet, hair all turned to white,
At blossom time goes back and forth a lot.

道上人房老梅　　　　　　p. 7b

孤高不受埃; 老怪昔誰栽
仙魄乘槎去; 龍身帶雪來
數枝寒照水; 一點淨沾苔
頭白狂詩客; 花時屢往囘

85 | PRESENTED TO THE RETIRED SCHOLAR TENG

I knew you, sir, at the time of war and trouble:
Now, it is over ten years since.
Among lakes and rivers, you have found a resting place,
And so you've now gone into hermitage.
Fresh breezes sweep your hut on its three acres;
Daylight spent with a benchful of books.
Leisurely days—your gateway always closed . . .
Even the neighboring monks cannot compare!

贈滕處士　　　　　　p. 7b

識君戎馬際; 今又十年餘
湖海纔安息; 先生便隱居
清風三畝宅; 白晝一床書
閒日門長掩; 隣僧亦不如

102

86 | WAKING FROM A DREAM

On my pillow, a dream of Master Zhuang!
I wake—the sun's reached afternoon.
I boil water from Cinnabar Well,
Brew tea from monks on a sacred mountain.
Last night's rain has lessened the flowers' spirit;
Thunder crashes lengthened the sprouting reeds.
My hometown is distant, at a corner of the ocean:
From far I think of it, in the midst of flowery spring.

Master Zhuang, or Zhuangzi, the great Daoist philosopher of the
fourth century BC, famously dreamed he was a butterfly, but on
awakening could not tell if he were the man, Zhuangzi, who had
dreamed of being a butterfly, or a butterfly, now dreaming he
was Zhuangzi.

夢回   pp. 7b–8a

一枕莊生夢; 回來日未銜
自煎砂井水; 更煮岳僧茶
宿雨消花氣; 驚雷長荻芽
故山滄海角; 遥念在春華

87 | Sent to Monk Congshan

Several years now I have not seen you:
Master, you must be shut in behind your gate.
Incense fragrance at the ancient temple,
Autumn colors above the fivefold peaks.
In games of chess, which of the monks can match you?
Done playing your lute, cranes will share your peace.
When again will you come to visit,
To chant poems, and talk, here in the woods with me?

寄從善上人　　　　　p. 8a

數載不相見；師應長閉關
香烟前代寺；秋色五峯山
棋進僧誰敵；琴餘鶴共閒
幾時重過我；吟話此林間

88 | IMPROMPTU

Green trees, how thick they flourish!
Fresh gusts of wind—true surplus here.
Pillow wrapped round by cloudy slivers,
Curtains penetrated by rainy spray.
Bamboo pipes bring spring water from the gully,
Lost stelae are unearthed by farmers' hoes.
In these mountains—how many have been the changes?
Men "plowed and farmed," learned "pottery and fishing."

It was sage Emperor Shun in antiquity who was said to have
"plowed, farmed, done pottery and fishing" as a youth, before
ascending to the throne; in other words, he was a humble man,
in touch with the lives of the farmers.

偶題   p. 8a

緑樹何稠疊；清風稍羨餘
枕縈雲片片；簾透雨踈踈
脩筧通泉塹；殘碑出野鋤
邱陵知幾變；耕稼學陶漁

89 | THE RESIDENCE OF A RECLUSE

The hundred affairs no longer work on you;
In the deserted wood—all day, your gate stands open.
Bees fly out, moistened with morning dew;
Cranes roost, breasting evening cloud.
The stones are ancient, moss becomes their face;
The pines are cold, creepers as their robes.
Mountain men and river men
Stop by to visit, lingering long.

隠者所居　　　　　　　　p. 8b

百事已無機; 空林不掩扉
蜂沾朝露出; 鶴帶晚雲歸
石老苔為貌; 松寒薜作衣
山翁與溪叟; 相過轉依依

90 | SEEING OFF MONK SHI ON AN ALMS TOUR

With your solitary cane, you leave the woods, and go:
Wind and frost will chill the road ahead.
Yourself you say, your karma, running out,
Has left you to enjoy this time of peace.
Floating leaves follow your Zen steps;
Hungry birds approach your field-dinners.
Back at your old hut, just the ancient Buddha:
No problem if folks come by for a look.

See poems 52 and 152 on the subject of fund-raising tours.

送奭公抄化　　　　　　　p. 8b

一錫出林去; 風霜前路寒
自言緣事了; 方得此身安
飄葉隨禪步; 饑禽傍野餐
舊房惟古佛; 來往任人看

91 | STAYING OVERNIGHT AT WUZI STOCKADE

I've already stopped at Dragon Lord's Shrine;
Morning after, crossed the lake at dawn.
Along the sandbanks, many boats are moored;
After fire, the land is mostly scorched.
Autumn has arrived—dusk stars all changed;
The sky so vast, moon over Chu, alone.
How desolate, stockaded village, far . . .
Try drafting men again—you won't find one.

宿鄔子寨下   p. 9a

已謁龍君廟; 明朝早過湖
傍沙船盡泊; 經火地多枯
秋至昏星易; 天長楚月孤
蕭條村戍濶; 更點有如無

92 | Presented to Zhao Lingxiu

A thousand mountains, leaves fallen in deep piles;
Towering trees no longer hide the birds.
The wanderer—where is he off to now?
His friend troubles his heart with thoughts of him.
Leisurely lamplight blocks off distant dreams;
Cold rain drowns out sad chanting of poems.
Monk Shi, remember, made this date with us:
When flowers bloom, to search for them together.

Zhao Lingxiu is Zhao Shixiu, fellow member of the Four Lings, all
of whom seems to be friends of Monk Shi (see 52, 90, and 181).

寄趙靈秀   p. 9a

千山落葉深；高樹不藏禽
游子在何處；故人勞此心
聞燈妨遠夢；寒雨亂愁吟
僧爽曽相約；花時共一尋

93 | MOORING OUR BOAT AT DRAGON-SWIM

Can't get the bridgemaster to open the locks—
We've gone ashore—not much freedom now!
Island birds fly into bamboo groves;
Mountain leaves fall in the river's flow.
Suddenly, autumn winds! We feel happy,
But then turn sad—the harvest premature!
Lying in bed, I hear the boatmen saying,
"Tomorrow, we should make it to Quzhou!"

泊舟龍游   pp. 9a–b

未得橋開鎖；去船難自由
渚禽飛入竹；山葉下隨流
忽見秋風喜；還成早歲愁
臥聞舟子説；明日到衢州

94 | STONE GATE HERMITAGE

Into the mountains, the deepest spot of all:
"Stone Gate" is the name of a cave there.
Mists rise like steam from the ruins of a deserted temple;
Snow presses, pure, on the little hermitage.
Fruits fall from trees—gathered by the gibbons;
Woods turn to darkness—a single tiger prowls.
There's just one monk: what can he achieve?
Seated in high meditation, as if without feeling at all.

石門菴   p. 10b

山到極深處；石門為洞名
嵐蒸空寺壞；雪壓小菴清
果落羣猿拾；林昏獨虎行
一僧何所得；高坐若無情

95 | PRESENTED TO SUN JIFAN

We stand and talk among the flying catkins,
Having met in the ruins of a palace of Wu.
And since I have been stupid in planning my life,
I feel for you, now your plans have also gone awry!
We drink, intoxicated by falling flowers in moonlight,
Chant bitter poems, bamboo swaying in the breeze.
I'll write my own "Lu Mountain Gazetteer,"
Wishing to explore every beauty spot here.

贈孫季蕃　　　　　　　　p. 10b

立談飛絮中；相遇在吳宮
以我為生拙；憐君失計同
醉酣花落月；吟苦竹搖風
自作廬山記；幽奇欲徧窮

96 | THE ZHOU FAMILY THATCHED HUT IN THE EASTERN GARDEN

In a corner of the town, where the old Xie village stood,
Survives this scholar's thatched hut.
All to be seen—mists and vapors rising;
Not the slightest sound of city noise.
Magpies come, and nest at tips of trees;
Turtles slide out, playing among roots of reeds.
All that's missing is a poet or two
To lean on these railings, and gaze upon these scenes.

周氏東山草堂　　　　　　p. 10b

城隅古謝村；博士草堂存
唯見烟霞起；全無市井喧
鵲來巢木末；黿出戲蒲根
消得吟詩客；憑欄看幾番

97 | TOGETHER WITH XU DAOHUI AND ZHAO ZISHI BOATING ON A LAKE

We met, and became friends on the spot!
How many chant on the poets' stage today?
Now in a little boat, this very day,
We enjoy at leisure the beautiful scenes we see.
Mountain rains increase the emerald colors;
Wind on the lake brings not one speck of dust.
Evening comes, and fishermen's songs arise:
Everywhere, the lotus bloom is fresh!

The poet describes an excursion with two other of the Four Lings, Xu Zhao and Zhao Shixiu.

同徐道暉趙紫芝泛湖   pp. 10b–11a

相見即相親；吟壇得幾人
扁舟當是日；勝賞共閒身
山雨曾添碧；湖風不動塵
晚來漁唱起；處處藕花新

98 | THE FASTING LADY

Still arrayed in her wedding garments,
Suddenly, she wished to pursue the Immortals.
All day long, she chants magic spells;
For one whole year, has only drunk stream water.
Her trim figure is not because she's sick;
Her strange utterances make folks think she's mad.
Should the Golden Mother learn what she's accomplished,
She'd invite her to enter the Heaven-Within-a-Cave.

This remarkable women is practicing the technique of "stopping
grains," that is, total fasting from all food while imbibing cosmic *qi* or
energy. The goal is to become a *xian*, or Immortal (see poem 71).

不食姑   p. 11b

嫁時衣尚著; 忽欲自尋仙
終日常持咒; 經年只飲泉
瘦形非是病; 怪語却如顛
金母還知爾; 招邀入洞天

99 | THE HOUSE OF SELF-SUFFICIENCY OF DAOIST ZHOU AT YULONG SHRINE

Those whose desires are never satiated
Would find it hard to share this residence.
Roasting on the brazier—"Young Maid" herbs ;
On the desk, the book of the "Old Master."
With flowers and bamboo the courtyard steps are freshened;
With wind-blown mists the windows are purified.
This man of Dao follows what lies beyond:
He sits here in peace, seeking nothing more.

The "Young Maid" (*chanu* 姹女) herb is a term used in Daoist
alchemy for mercury, or for herbs believed capable of transform-
ing into mercury, a key ingredient in the Elixir of immortality. The
"Old Master" would be Laozi, author of the *Daodejing*; "Lao"
according to most traditions was actually his surname, but the
poet purposely exploits the character's meaning of "old," to match
"young" in this parallel couplet.

玉隆宮周道士自足軒　　　　pp. 12a–b

貪得無厭者; 應難共此居
爐中姹女藥; 案上老君書
花竹庭階潔; 風烟户牖虛
道人随分外; 安坐不求餘

100 | Late in Autumn, Seeing Off Xu Ji to Take Up Duties as Aide at Longxi; On the Way, He Will Stop Off at His Old Residence at Quan'nan

Your scrolls are filled with "Airs" and "Elegances"
Hard for even famous writers to match!
In a remote town, you'll make a mere pittance;
But in another place, you'll visit your old hut.
Along the way, you'll mostly view chrysanthemums;
Half your luggage, baskets full of books.
So hard to believe that in this enlightened dynasty,
No one yet has presented your Zixu poem at court!

The "Airs" and "Elegances" are sections of the classic *Book of Songs* (*Shijing* 詩經), said to have been edited by Confucius and containing poems from as early as c. 1000 BCE. Zixu (子虛), literally "Master Emptiness," was the subject of a prose-poem by Sima Xiangru (Szu-ma Hsiangju 司馬相如, 179–117 BCE). His "Prose-poem on Master Emptiness" gained the poet fame when shown to Emperor Wu of the Han Dynasty. Wen Juan's poem is a subtle complaint that Xu Ji, another of the Four Lings, has not been adequately recognized.

晚秋送徐璣赴龍溪丞因過泉南舊里　　p. 12b

卷中風雅句; 名匠亦難如
遠邑親微禄; 他鄉過舊廬
程途多見菊; 行李半擔書
未信文明代; 無人薦子虛

101 | MOORING DURING A BOAT TRIP

Several days now, in my boat's cabin on the river;
Blinds hanging down, thwarted by river conditions.
Happily, we are moored at a mountain town;
I like walking along the riverbanks.
As I stroll, I hear a flute playing—homesickness rises;
Gazing at pine trees, desires for officialdom fade.
And I know that far away, this very moon
Is shining clearly upon my hometown.

旅泊   p. 12b

幾日溪篷下；低垂困水程
喜因山縣泊；暑向岸汀行
聞笛生覊思；看松減宦情
遥知此夜月；必照故山明

102 | THE JUNIPER AT THE ANCIENT SHRINE AT
CHANGZHOU

What man planted this juniper?
Tradition says it was Dugu Ji.
Years passed, it became a treasure,
Name entered in the local gazetteers.
Its old knots so solid, hard for bugs to bore;
Wrinkled bark split, appearing as if withered.
It has established roots beside the shrine of a great emperor:
It has nothing to fear from woodcutters here.

Dugu Ji (Tugu Chi 獨孤及, 725–77) was a Tang Dynasty official.

常州古廟檜   p. 13a

此檜何人植；相傳是獨孤
年深成古物；名重入州圖
老節堅難蠹；皺皮裂似枯
託根烈帝廟；應不慮樵夫

103 | BAMBOO

Just happened to plant you to get some shade:
You flourished fully, surpassing the other trees.
When moonlight is cold, there a pair of doves sleep;
When winds die down, there one cicada sings.
Reflected below, your colors enhance the moss's green;
Overhanging the pond, you make the water seem deeper.
Living here in poverty, few visitors ever come:
I rely on you to console my heart.

竹　　　　　　　　　　　p. 13b

偶種得成陰；翛翛過別林
月寒雙鴿睡；風静一蟬吟
映地添苔碧；臨池覺水深
貧居來客少；賴爾慰人心

104 | STUDYING IN A MOUNTAIN TEMPLE, SENT TO INQUIRE OF MY CITY FRIENDS

I brought along just a basket of books,
And sit reading all day long in the deserted woods.
Whenever I see the monks about their business,
The mind of serenity arises within.
Empty pavilion—cloud-slivers moor here;
Slanting pathways—tree roots invade.
It's not really that far from the city walls:
If you have a moment's leisure, come chant poems with me.

讀書山寺寄問城間諸友　　pp. 13b–14a

止攜書一篋；長日坐空林
每見僧家事；便生靜者心
虛亭雲片泊；仄徑樹根侵
去郭無多地；閒來相對吟

105 | Taking to the Road after Clearing

Clear skies now—remaining moisture still:
Tree after tree, glistening with emerald light.
A hungry egret stands peering at the stream;
A lazy boy lies sleeping on an ox.
Somewhere in the mountain, I know there's a temple,
But fear that there's no boat to cross the stream.
Cut stones have newly laid out a pathway:
Names of famous men inscribed on the stones.

初晴道中 　　　　　　　pp. 15a–b

初晴餘濕在; 樹樹碧光鮮
饑鷺窺泉立; 頑童跨犢眠
依山知有寺; 過水恨無船
砌石新成路; 芳名石上鐫

106 | PRESENTED TO NOBLE SCHOLAR LIU

Of immortal realms, Mount Lu is supreme:
This is where the Noble Scholar makes his home.
This excursion has led me to reside in the capital,
But here's one who's exchanged all that for mountain mists!
In search of verses, we encounter wild cranes;
Sutras in hand, we sit and face the flowers.
Our lively discussion not yet at an end,
We rise, and see the Jade Rope Stars slanting across the sky.

贈劉高士   p. 14b

仙境康廬最；高人此處家
今游住京國；誰代管烟霞
覓句行逢鶴；持經坐對花
快談方未已；起看玉繩斜

107 | THINGS HAPPENING NOW

I drink a bit, but can't get drunk:
Lonely sadness—what is there to do?
Evening mists half mingle with the clouds;
Spring snow is mixing with the rain.
The flowers are wet, few people pass that way;
The sky is cold, many the cries of geese.
I lean on the railing, feelings limitless,
Yearning for the past, singing in aimless grief.

即事   pp. 15a–b

小飲不成醉；牢愁將奈何
晚烟雲半雜；春雪雨相和
花濕人行少；空寒雁叫多
凭闌思無極；懷古謾悲歌

108 | Late Spring–Retiring in Illness

With every morning, new scenes now appear;
Sick as I am, I still raise the blinds.
I wash my herbs, dry them near the flowers;
Transmitted prescriptions paste up on the wall.
Strength failing, I cut down on my speech;
Body aging, keep eyes on my beard.
Yesterday, a monk came from the woods:
For the first time, I picked up a cup of tea.

暮春病歸   p. 15b

朝朝風景添; 吾病亦開簾
洗藥花前曬; 傅方壁上黏
力微還省語; 身老更看髯
昨日林僧至; 茶杯始一拈

109 | WALKING IN THE MOONLIGHT ON THE MID-AUTUMN FESTIVAL

Mysterious feelings tug mercilessly:
Along the river I walk, and walk some more.
No way of knowing how many people
Have been deeply moved by this moon tonight!
The brilliance compels the fireflies to halt;
The coldness invades and startles nesting birds.
I want to return, but still cannot bear to:
Pure dew drips through the Third Watch.

The Third Watch is from 11 pm to 1 am.

中秋步月　　　　　　　　p. 16a

幽興苦相引；水邊行復行
不知今夜月；曾動幾人情
光逼流螢斷；寒侵宿鳥驚
欲歸猶未忍；清露滴三更

110 | LAMENTING THE DEATH OF CHAN MASTER JIN

You became enlightened to the mystery of Non-Birth,
Now return unto the Void as to your home.
In your bamboo dwelling, a three-foot image;
On your stone bed a single stick of incense.
Your tattered monk's robe still hangs from a tree;
The newly planted pine has suddenly surged above the wall.
Unable to remain in the realm of the monks,
For how many days will it be desolate here?

悼瑾公禪師   p. 16a

了悟無生妙; 歸空若故鄉
竹房三尺像; 石榻一爐香
壞衲猶懸樹; 新松忽過墻
僧中留不得; 幾日為淒涼

111 | THINGS HAPPENING NOW–EXPRESSING MY FEELINGS

I've written about my eccentric nature,
Which surely leads my traces far away.
The only friends I have are rustic guests,
And what we talk about is poetry.
Listening to rain, I sleep in monks' quarters;
Watching clouds, stand on a fishing raft.
Autumn comes—I write new verses,
Most of them about chrysanthemums.

即事言懷   p. 17a

賦得迂踈性; 合令踪跡賒
相親惟野客; 所論是詩家
聽雨眠僧屋; 看雲立釣槎
秋來有新句; 多半為黃花

112 | Nengren Temple

Lotus Blossom Peak pierces the sky;
The temple is connected to the peak.
I've gotten at last to see this winter moon:
I've wanted to come here for years and years!
In the cold pond trembles the pagoda's reflection;
Ancient trees are filled with kitchen smoke.
I happen to see a noble monk emerge:
On his meditation bench, he sits in utter silence.

能仁寺　　　　　　　　pp. 17a–b

芙蓉峯入天; 寺與此峯連
得見是冬月; 要來從昔年
寒潭搖塔影; 古木帶厨烟
偶值高僧出; 禪牀坐默然

113 | Presented to Monk Yue of the Eastern Hermitage

I ask your age: just eighty years old now:
Retired to this cloister, serenity for so long.
White snow—too lazy to trim your whiskers;
Green pines—closing your door early at night.
You get stream water to brew your tea,
With guests, discuss excursions to climb mountains.
Which of these monks are your disciples?
—So many black robes, coming and going here!

贈東庵約公　　　　　　p. 17b

問年今八十; 退院久清閑
白雪髭慵剃; 青松户早關
取泉來煮茗; 與客話遊山
弟子何僧是; 緇衣多往還

114 | A Funeral Lament for Chen Xilao's Mother

Reaching the great age of over eighty,
Living in widowhood, having suffered your full share.
To maintain your household, you had no one else,
Just this one son, who became a poet.
Travelers afar send letters of condolence;
Your new tomb has Buddhas as neighbors.
In the autumn chamber, your portrait is hanging:
Gaunt visage, just the way you were alive.

Chen Xilao was a close friend of the Four Lings and a fellow poet (see 180).

陳西老母氏挽詞　　　　p. 18a

八十餘年壽; 孀居備苦辛
成家無別物; 有子作詩人
遠客遺書弔; 新墳得佛隣
秋堂挂遺像; 癯若在時身

115 | SEEING OFF OLD MAN WENG YING ON HIS RETURN TO FUJIAN

I meet you, sir, also surnamed "Weng:"
Is it possible that we are relatives?
You've come from Thorn Tree village
To visit the Jade Cauldron Peak.
Although we may have met each other late,
It seems as if our friendly love runs deep.
Now, down the road swept by autumn winds,
How far will you enter the Fujian mountains?

送翁應叟歸閩   p. 18b

逢君亦姓翁; 莫即是吾宗
遠自刺桐里; 來看玉甑峯
雖云相識晚; 宛若故情濃
囘首秋風路; 閩山復幾重

116 | HUANGBO TEMPLE IN FUZHOU

In the world, there are two Huangbo Temples:
This one here is the original!
The stelae bear witness to visitors of former ages,
Among the monks, I encounter countrymen.
I stay overnight, rain outside the Zen chambers;
When I pass on, again, dust of the traveler's road.
Before departure, again I pay my respects
To the bodies of the Twelve Patriarchs here.

福州黃蘗寺   pp. 18b–19a

天下兩黃蘗; 此中山是真
碑看前代客; 僧值故鄉人
一宿禪房雨; 經時客路塵
將行更瞻禮; 十二祖師身

117 | MOURNING FOR MOUNTAIN CITIZEN XU

Already, suffering had penetrated your bones:
But who would have thought you would die so soon?
Clearly, the Creator of Creatures intends
To crush those who work hard at poetry!
Flower colors extend across the clear-skied day;
Warblers' songs are heard from all around.
Who made this three-foot portrait of you,
Still showing your spirit of gaunt purity?

"Mountain Citizen Xu" was Xu Zhao of the Four Lings, known to
have died in 1211.

哭徐山民   p. 19a

已是窮侵骨；何期早喪身
分明造物意；磨折苦吟人
花色連晴晝；鶯聲在近隣
誰令三尺像；猶帶瘦精神

118 | Inscribed on the Forest Pavilion of Administrator Zhao of Wuyi

It seems all the beauty spots of Wu Stream
Are spread out before your eaves!
Sun gleaming over towers and terraces of the town,
Mist floating through mulberries of the villages.
Birds sing, spring fills the valley;
Rice-sprouts turn green, paddies brimming with water.
So rich with woodcutter and fisherman scenes,
My poem cannot possibly sing of them all!

題武義趙提幹林亭   p. 19a

武溪諸勝狀；如列在簷前
一郭樓臺日；數村桑柘烟
鳥啼春滿谷；秧緑水平田
饒有漁樵景；吾詩詠不全

119 | Along South Stream Seeking Han Zhongzhi, but Unable to Find Him

Tree after tree with lovely shade,
Mountain cicadas, chirping without a stop.
I cup some water from the southern stream:
As pure as the owner's heart!
Above the house, clouds scud coldly;
At roots of hedges, lichens grow thick.
I leave my poem inscribed on the cliff:
Tomorrow, I will search for him again.

南澗尋韓仲止不遇   p. 19b

樹樹有佳陰；山蟬不住吟
掬來南澗水；清若主人心
屋上雲飛冷；籬根蘚積深
留詩在巖壁；明日更相尋

120 | MOURNING FOR XU JI

Last time, returning from official duties,
With great grief, I lost Linghui.
Who would have thought that three years later,
The ten-thousand transformations would take you as well?
The pagoda-slope extends to your tomb;
Pond colors face your house's door.
Never again will you put on the sandals of leisure,
To visit monks, and watch them play games of chess.

Linghui (Xu Zhao), had already died in 1211 (see 117). Xu Ji
followed in 1214, providing a *terminus post quem* for Weng
Juan's death.

哭徐璣   pp. 20a–b

前時官上歸；感愴失靈暉

不料三年後；俱随萬化非

塔峯長入座；池色自臨扉

無復乘閒屐；觀棋訪衲衣

121 | Presented to Retired Scholar Bao

Day after day, along the lake's shore,
Flocks of gulls are your companions.
Your entire household loves the Buddha;
Alone, you sit, perhaps watching mountains.
You dry out herbs, worried when rain clouds come,
Go out with monks to enjoy the moon.
And sometimes, you get in a little boat,
Arriving in moments at the town!

贈鮑居士   p. 20b

日日湖波畔；羣鷗相共閒
全家皆好佛；獨坐或看山
曬藥嫌雲住；留僧伴月還
有時乘小艇；忽爾到城間

122 | A Friend Who Lives in the Woods

Flowers, rocks, and your hut in the woods:
None would be chosen by vulgar men!
You spread sand to soften the pathways,
Use bamboo to form hedgelike rows.
Guests stay over to share family dinners;
You teach your sons to recite from ancient books.
You always say, the way to lead one's life
Is simple: be like woodcutters and fishermen.

友人林居   p. 20b

花石與林廬；皆非俗者居
鋪沙為徑軟；因竹夾籬疎
留客同家食；教兒誦古書
常言治生意；只欲似樵漁

123 | THINGS HAPPENING AT JINGKOU

The lower reaches of the Yangzi River:
"Iron Archway" one of the towns here.
So many famous ruins of former years:
The man of leisure wishes to see them all.
In setting sunlight, temples above the ripples;
In bright moonlight, towers of the stockade.
One tune floats from a fisherman's flute
And moves me to endless sadness.

京口即事　　　　　　　p. 21a

長江當下流；鐵甕此為州
前代多名迹；閒人欲遍遊
夕陽波上寺；明月戍邊樓
一曲漁家笛；生予無限愁

124 | Presented to Alchemist Jiao

Beside the pines you shut your gate,
Just returned from selling medicines.
You teach visitors to recognize immortal herbs;
Laugh at those who seek the "purple robe."
You love your lute so much, you sleep with it;
You read the *Book of Changes*, but cite it rarely.
I hear you find Yuansha a vulgar place:
Fully at leisure, perhaps you'll fly away.

The alchemist is named Li 李 in a variant edition. The "purple robe" is given by Emperors as a special honor to Buddhist monks or Daoist practitioners.

贈焦鍊師   p. 21a

松邊自掩扉; 賣藥罷方歸
教客認仙草; 笑人求紫衣
惜琴眠處放; 玩易語時稀
見說沅砂賤; 閒身去欲飛

125 | INSCRIBED ON ALCHEMIST WANG'S RESIDENCE

There must be many Immortals who visit here,
To see you at peace in your magic grotto.
Moonlit creepers grow longer in spring;
Wind-swept bamboo with evening breathe out chill.
Beneath your seal, ghosts and demons are quelled;
In your cauldron, dragon and tiger joyfully merge.
Way beyond all ordinary karma,
You spend your time reading unorthodox books.

"Dragon and tiger" are the yang and yin forces that the alchemist
strives to combine to produce the Elixir.

題王法師房   p. 29a

應有列仙至; 觀當靈洞安
月蘿春長蔓; 風竹暮生寒
印下鬼神役; 鼎交龍虎歡
尋常應緣外; 多把異書看

126 | SEEKING A MONK

Autumn purity, sun so brilliant;
Walking at leisure, breeze filling my robe.
Seeking a monk, but never finding him,
I pluck one chrysanthemum, and return.

尋僧   p. 25a

秋净日暉暉; 閒行風滿衣
尋僧雖不遇; 折得菊花歸

127 | EARLY PLUM BLOSSOMS OUTSIDE MY HOUSE

I've walked to every river village,
    no plum trees could I find!
Now suddenly, a single blossom
    opens in the warm grove here.
How did the yellow bees find out
    the lately breaking news?
They've tracked the fragrance from next door,
    flying into my yard.

舍外早梅   p. 25b

行遍江村未有梅; 一花忽向暖林開
黃蜂何處知消息; 便解尋香隔舍來

128 | AUTUMN FEELINGS

No matter whether autumn skies
    be cloudy or be clear,
When do autumn feelings fail
    to pierce me to the quick?
Over the river city, so many
    nights without a moon,
And so I've written poems inspired
    by the falling rains.

秋懷   pp. 26b–27a

不管秋天陰復晴; 秋懷何處不淒清
江城幾夜無佳月; 亦有新詩對雨成

129 | RUSTIC VIEW

A whole sky of autumn color,
    chilling the clear bay:
Innumerable peaks and mountains
    far away and near.
Leisurely I climb the mountains
    to gaze down at the water,
And—suddenly—down in the water
    I see verdant mountains!

野望   p. 27a

一天秋色冷晴灣; 無數峯巒遠近間
閒上山來看野水; 忽於水底見青山

130 | In Spring Climbing Nanchang City Wall

Alone I climb the river city's wall,
      gazing all around:
In this scene, there's not one thing
      unworthy of a poem!
To learn how far along the spring
      has gotten in this place,
Just note the greenery of the plants,
      not yet all uniform.

春登南昌城   p. 27b

獨上江城四望低; 望中無物不堪題

欲知春事幾深淺; 芳草青青猶未齊

131 | Master Feng's Ridge

Wild peaks, a thousand layers
      brushing clouds and rainbows;
Spokes joined together—valleys, cliffs
      rising like a ladder . . .
Once I saw a scene like this,
      near the town of Kuozhou:
But all those mountains would have been
      much lower than this ridge.

馮公嶺   pp. 59a–b

亂峯千疊拂雲霓; 輻合坑崖立似梯

曾向括州州裏望; 衆山却是此山低

132 | MOUNTAIN RAIN

All night long, throughout the woods,
    the stars and moon shine clear.
There is not the slightest bit of cloud,
    no thunder sounds at all.
At crack of dawn, quite suddenly,
    the swollen stream flows by:
I realize this was rain that fell
    in another mountain range.

山雨　　　　　　　p. 29b

一夜滿林星月白; 且無雲氣亦無雷
平明忽見溪流急; 知是他山落雨來

133 | Sent to "Mountain Man" Xu Linghui

Just separated by mist and cloud,
    a distance of few miles,
We once agreed we'd travel together
    to enjoy these hidden scenes.
How could we know our untrammeled wings
    would fly in opposite directions?
Just as I am entering the mountains,
    you are going out!

Another poem addressed to fellow Four Lings member Xu Zhao.

寄山人徐靈暉   p. 29b

只隔烟霞數里間; 本期還往共幽閒
寧知逸羽飛相背; 我入山來君出山

134 | FOURTH MONTH IN A COUNTRY VILLAGE

Green covers the mountain fields,
  white fills the streams;
Embraced by songs of cuckoo birds,
  the rainfall is like mist.
The country village, in the fourth month,
  has few folks taking rest:
As soon as they're done with silkworm tasks,
  they start to plant the rice.

This has become the most frequently anthologized poem by
Weng Juan, even included in anthologies of classical poems
for children.

鄉村四月   p. 30a

緑遍山原白滿川; 子規聲裡雨如烟
鄉村四月閒人少; 纔了蠶桑又插田

Ink painting of Huangshan, the Yellow Mountains, by Shitao (Shih T'ao 石濤, ca. 1642–1707), dated 1670. Poem 141 describes Xu Zhao parting with a friend returning to his home there, remarkable evidence that by the time of Shi-tao's painting the Yellow Mountains had been known as a place of reclusion and alchemical practice for more than five centuries.

36 POEMS BY XU ZHAO

(Linghui 靈暉, d. 1211)

Page numbers refer to the one-chapter collected works of Xu Zhao, "Collection from the Studio of Fragrant Orchids" (*Fanglanxuan ji* 芳蘭軒集), in the *Siku quanshu*.

135 | In the distribution of themes, I got "Evening Glow over the Fishing Village"

The fisherman has caught his fish,
    and sold them round the streams;
His little boat is tied athwart
    outside the bramble gate.
His old wife emerges from the door,
    shoos the chickens and dogs;
She gathers up his hat and coat,
    hangs them to dry from the eaves.
Having sold his fish,
    he's gotten wine and also cash to spare:
Back home now, he falls down, drunk,
    and sleeps right on the ground.
The little children clamber to know
    when the rice will be ready;
White gulls go flying off
    through mist above reed flowers.

Poetic themes would be distributed by the host to the guests at
a literary gathering. From this the poet created a vivid scene from
the fisherman's life, with which he seems to be familiar (see 146).

分題得漁村晚照　　　　　p. 5a

漁師得魚繞溪賣; 小船橫繫柴門外
出門老嫗喚鷄犬; 收斂蓑衣屋頭曬
賣魚得酒又得錢; 歸來醉倒地上眠
小兒啾啾問煮米; 白鷗飛去蘆花烟

136 | PRESENTED TO MONK QIN OF THE RIVER-CENTER TEMPLE

A visitor arrives, opens the hidden door;
His bamboo-shoot sandals wander winding corridors.
Tides invade your meditation stone;
Rain dampens your sutra-reading candle.
Your ancient inkstone, a gift from someone far;
New bamboo grows higher than the pagoda.
In the city now it is hot as burning fire;
Here, it is still pure and cool.

贈江心寺欽上人　　　　p. 5b

客至啟幽户; 笋鞋行曲廊
潮侵坐禪石; 雨潤讀經香
古硯傳人遠; 新篁過塔長
城中如火熱; 此地獨清凉

137 | PRESENTED TO LIU MINGYUAN

Your whole life you've despised worldly vulgarity,
Never residing in any city.
And since you haven't "plucked the cassia,"
You're willing to reside with fishermen.
For illness you take the old Zen Master's medicine;
Your poems respond to letters from rustic men.
You speak as well of refining the Elixir:
I'm shamed my life cannot compare with yours.

To "pluck the cassia," which grows on the moon in Chinese folk-lore, means to pass the top civil service examination.

贈劉明遠　　　　p. 6a

一生嫌世俗; 不向市中居
既是未攀桂; 却堪同釣魚
疾除禪老藥; 詩答野人書
又說成丹鼎; 吾生愧不如

141

138 | STAYING OVERNIGHT AT A TEMPLE

Ancient halls, chilly in pure lamplight;
Deserted corridors, leaves swept by wind.
Gates shut, beyond all human traces;
Verses come with the Buddhas' incense.
Cranes are sleeping; surely they have no dreams;
Monks are conversing, they must be enlightened on the Void.
Seated here, I'm astonished at dawn breaking in the window,
A crescent moon still east of the wood.

宿寺   p. 7a

古殿清燈冷；虛廊葉掃風
撐關人迹外；得句佛香中
鶴睡應無夢；僧談必悟空
坐驚窗欲曉；片月在林東

139 | INSCRIBED ON THE OLD RESIDENCE OF LUO YIN

A swath of stream so pure, no speck of dust;
Green mountains, neighbors on all four sides.
Heaven above seems to have intended
That this would be a place for a poet.
The things he sang of are all gone now;
And fate decreed he should live in poverty.
So I have have come in search of ancient traces:
All I see is a rock, shaped like a unicorn.

Luo Yin (Lo Yin 羅隱, c 833–910) was an important late-Tang poet.

題羅隱故居   pp. 7a–b

片水靜無塵；青山是四隣
上天如有意；此地著詩人
吟得物俱盡；罰令生世貧
因來尋古跡；只見石為麟

140 | INSCRIBED ON THE SHRINE OF THE PEACH BLOSSOM LADY

On one tree, peach blossoms bloom:
These peach blossoms are actually *you.*
A deserted pond overlooks rustic streams:
Where are scudding clouds to be sought?
Your doings are discussed by the woodcutters here;
Incense is burned by passers-by.
Rains add moss to your epitaph:
So hard to read the text of these ancient poems!

The title refers to a great beauty of antiquity, whom poets have written about down through the centuries. Like many historical figures, she was apotheosized and shrines built in her memory. The burning of incense in her honor is a religious act, praying for her protection. Xu Zhao has captured the way in which great historical personages or happenings are kept alive not only by poets and scholars, but by ordinary people of the region.

題桃花夫人廟   p. 7b

一樹桃花發；桃花即是君
空池臨野水；何處覓行雲
事迹樵人説；爐香過客焚
雨添碑上蘚；難讀古詩文

141 | SEEING OFF LI WEI ON HIS RETURN TO THE YELLOW MOUNTAINS

Mind harmonious, no white hairs,
Always bringing along your lute you travel.
How long a journey until you reach your home?
Many peaks face the county seat.
Wife and kids are poor, and yet they're happy;
Elixir, herbs each year you roast and complete.
You don't need an enlightened era:
You've ended known for your life of reclusion.

An early reference to a life of reclusion in the Yellow Mountains
of Anhui Province, whose great reputation will only occur in late
Ming-early Qing (mid-17th century). See illustration, p. 138

送李偉歸黃山　　　　　p. 7b

心和無白髮; 長帶一琴行
幾路到君屋; 數峰當郡城
妻兒貧自樂; 丹藥歲燒成
未必聖明代; 終令隱姓名

142 | Paying a Visit to Master Guan and not Finding Him at Home

The resting dog, hearing me, runs out;
Your gateway faces an oak-tree grove.
Of course I know you are often away,
Yet from far I've come in search of you.
The evening seems short, lingering incense rises from the seal;
Neighbors are scattered, but sounds of chimes emerge.
Recently you sent tea,
Probably worried I worked too hard at poetry.

An "incense seal" is burning, a device whose openings for releasing incense fumes are cut in characters conveying poetry or religious texts. They may also function as clocks. See Silvio A. Bedini, *The Trail of Time: Time Measurement with Incense in East Asia* (Cambridge University Press, 2005). The chimes indicate the presence of nearby Buddhist temples.

訪觀公不遇　　　　　　p. 8a

卧犬聞人出；門當青櫟林
固知多不在；自遠欲相尋
宵短餘香印；鄰踈出磬音
昨來曾寄茗；應念苦吟心

143 | WITHERING WILLOWS

Winds have buffeted them—not one catkin left;
Never again their blue-green nesting-places.
The branches are fragile after the frosty chill;
The roots with no soil slip into the stream's waves.
In the cold, egrets come to roost early;
In the darkness, wild insects throng.
Beyond this abandoned garden and overgrown embankment
Men lament the passing of their old beauty.

衰柳   p. 8b

風吹無一葉；不復翠成窠
枝脆經霜氣；根空入水波
寒棲江鷺早；暗出野螢多
廢苑荒堤外；人嗟舊跡過

144 | EGRETS

Single dots of white like snow,
Crowns with a few silk threads attached,
They leave their footprints along the sandy shore,
Then depart through the void without a sound
Only in tall willows are their nests secure;
In dangerous rapids they stand without fear.
I always notice their serenity of mind:
In former lives they must have been fishermen.

鷺鷥   p. 8b

一點白如雪；頂黏絲數莖
沙邊行有跡；空外過無聲
高柳巢方穩；危灘立不驚
每看閒意思；漁父是前生

145 | CLIMBING TO MOUNT SHE TEMPLE

Stone pathway, nearly falling off;
Only at the top does it straighten out.
My steps are halted by lovely flowers and trees;
Chanting poems, I don't notice the monks' welcome.
On the front side, there's no stream at the gate;
The road from the eastern corner leads to the capital.
Green peaks, Thirty-Six of them:
On frosty mornings you see them clearly.

The Yellow Mountains, where or near which this temple is located,
is famed for its Thirty-Six Peaks, although there actually are a
great deal more.

登歙山寺   pp. 8b–9a

石徑半欹傾；山頭路始平
步因花樹息；吟忘寺僧迎
一面門無水；東隅路入京
青峰三十六；霜曉見分明

146 | FISHERMAN'S FAMILY

The fisherman has grown old,
His livelihood all in fishing lines.
Along this remote stream, no one else has settled,
His little boat he can paddle anywhere.
Several fish on fresh willow-wood skewers,
A single flute, played by his young son.
When he has wine, the whole family gets drunk:
Has he ever wished to meet with high officials?

漁家　　　　　　　p. 9a

阿翁年紀老; 生計在綸絲
野水無人占; 扁舟逐處移
數鱗新柳串; 一笛小兒吹
有酒全家醉; 公卿要識誰

147 | ACTUAL SCENES IN THE MOUNTAINS

He puts on clogs to climb the steep slopes,
Cries out to the boy, "Careful with those clay cups!"
A thousand escarpments have passed through rain;
A single wild goose brings autumn in with him.
In rustic skiff, they set out on the lake;
Owners of mountain gardens welcome him in.
The rest of his life spent with woodcutters and shepherds,
His gate, the alleyway have few specks of dust.

山中即事　　　　　p. 9a

著屐上崔嵬; 呼兒注瓦杯
千岑經雨後; 一鴈帶秋來
野艇乘湖發; 山園逐主開
餘生落樵牧; 門巷少塵埃

148 | THE WATERFALL AT STONE GATE

A single stream falling from the heavens:
It surely once was seen by Li Po!
For thousands of years it has flowed and never run out,
Even in the sixth month the place is always cold.
Splashing against trees, tiny bubbles leap forth;
Striking rock it turns angry turbulence.
Folks here say, from the deep blue pool below
An old dragon often coils up.

Although it is not known whether they traveled together, at some point all four Lings visited and wrote verse about this remote Stone Gate retreat, with its single monk in residence and impressive waterfall (see 4, 94, 156, and 184). Here Xu Zhao surmises that the famous Tang poet Li Po (more popularly Li Bai 李白, 701–762) likely visited four centuries earlier.

石門瀑布　　　　　　　　　p. 9b

一泒從天下；曾經李白看
千年流不盡；六月地長寒
灑木跳微沫；衝崖作怒湍
人言深碧處；常有老龍盤

149 | INSCRIBED ON THE WALL OF STONE CLIFF TEMPLE AT QUZHOU

A stone sticks out from shore, diverts the flow;
This stream runs one mile through the level wood.
Clustered boats in cold all cross together;
At the towering temple, distant mountains match.
Lingering chimes, wafted by wind, now stop;
Sleeping birds weigh the bamboo low.
One thing I'm sad for: darkness so intense
It's hard to read the poems on the walls.

題衢州石壁寺   p. 10a

岸石橫生脈；平林一里溪
衆船寒渡集；高寺遠山齊
殘磬吹風斷；眠禽壓竹低
自嫌昏黑至；難認壁間題

150 | YEARNING FOR ZHAO ZIZHI

Since we parted, a hundred days have passed,
No letters from you in all that time!
How many nights have I dreamed of you?
Alone, I've given up chanting autumn poems.
Slight snow, but clothes still heavy;
Poor harvest—rice worth its weight in gold..
"Those who know one's music" do exist,
But how can they compare to you, who know my heart?

Zhao Zishi refers to fellow Ling member Zhao Shixiu.

懷趙紫芝   p. 13a

一別一百日；無書直至今
幾回成夜夢；獨自廢秋吟
小雪衣猶紛；荒年米似金
知音人亦有；誰若爾知心

151 | PRESENTED TO ALCHEMIST LI OF NINE FLOWERS MOUNTAIN

I'll always recall how at Ling-ling Commandery
Together we'd view the peaks along the river.
Your whole life you've despised the events of this world;
In how many places did you discover traces of Immortals?
Now you've turned to controlling thunder, lightning,
And imprinting seals that subdue tigers and dragons.
Eleven-hundred miles between us—
Yet today, once again we meet!

The great interest in alchemy of the Four Lings is demonstrated by their poems to masters of the art. Weng Juan composed three poems presented to various alchemists (see 80, 124, 125), the first of those also to one "Alchemist Li," while Zhao Shixiu discussed herbs and elixirs in several poems (34, 46, and 63) as did Xu Ji (178).

贈九華李丹士　　　　　　　　p. 13a

長記零陵郡; 共看江上峯
一生輕世事; 幾處認仙蹤
轉式驅雷電; 封泥伏虎龍
三千三百里; 今日又相逢

152 | SEEING OFF MONK SHI ON A FUND-RAISING TRIP

With focused purpose, your affairs always succeed;
And so I expect on this undertaking.
The tower will be splendid, with images of numinous beings;
A stele shall record the donors' names.
The river here is broad, winds urge your crossing;
The village lies deep in snow, thwarting your departure.
Brief respite to painstaking work, we speak together
And I'm able to see you off in relaxed mood.

See also poems 52 and 90 on the subject of fund-raising trips.

送奭上人化緣　　　　　pp. 13a–b

專志事皆成; 期師此一行
閣盛靈物像; 碑載施人名
江濶風催渡; 村深雪廢程
暫勞曾共說; 終可送閒情

153 | INSCRIBED ON THE WALL OF THE MELON HUT OF XUE JINGSHI

Where can one find a melon hut?
On this calm lake of over four acres.
Yourself you hoe away weeds from the furrows
Without dropping the book held in you hand.
Folks from afar come seeking your calligraphy;
The boy gets time off, goes out to fish.
A mountain man resides up in the mountains—
He envies you your living by the water!

See poem 27 for more for on the "melon hut" as a metaphor
for retirement.

題薛景石瓜廬　　　　　　p. 13b

何地有瓜廬；平湖四畝餘
自鋤畦上草；不放手中書
人遠來求字；童閒去釣魚
山民山上住；却羨水邊居

154 | THE WATERFALL AT DRAGON POND

It flies straight down a thousand feet,
Nowhere with any fixed form.
Lightning flashes, shot from heaven's sun;
A dragon leaps up, stone-born clouds spread its odor.
This powerful thrust I have viewed in spring;
Its cold roar is listened to by the Buddhas.
Men of the past have told us that
Washing eyes in this water improves your sight.

龍湫瀑布　　　　　　　　p. 14a

飛下數千尺；全然無定形
電橫天日射；龍出石雲腥
壯勢春曾看；寒聲佛共聽
昔人云此水；洗目最能靈

155 | SOUL PEAK

I've come, speechless at the scene,
At leisure recognizing former traces.
But who planted these path-side trees?
They block the view of the summit!
The pond's gone dry, exposing sunken rocks;
I stand, avoiding being struck by departing birds!
Woodcutters speak of a dangerous Bridge of the Immortals,
And I think, this place might be an altar.

靈峰　　　　　　　　　p. 14a

我來無一語；閒認昔遊蹤
誰種路旁樹；却遮山上峯
潭乾沈石露；人立去禽衝
樵説仙橋險；因思在上封

156 | STONE GATE HERMITAGE

How many years back was this hermitage built?
Now there just one monk who lives in it.
These gray cliffs, sheer, have been here since antiquity;
Even in broad daylight few people attempt the climb.
All things here form a lovely whole,
But my life? Reclusion is impossible.
Last night a new tiger must have passed:
Claws have torn the vines at the base of the tree.

石門菴　　　　　　　　p. 14b

庵是何年作；其中住一僧
蒼崖從古險；白日少人登
衆物清相映；吾生隱未能
夜來新過虎；抓折樹根藤

157 | INSCRIBED ON THE MOUNTAIN RESIDENCE OF WENG JUAN

Ten years ago, we made a vow of reclusion;
Now, I still live in the city!
I envy your ability to take your children by the hand
And deep in the mountains build yourself a hut.
You've changed the stream's course with stones near the bank,
Planted herbs among the garden vegetables.
And you tell me that beyond this towering forest,
Woodcutters hear you chanting from your books.

題翁卷山居   p. 14b–15a

十年前有約；今却在城居
羨爾能攜子；深山自結廬
引泉移岸石；栽藥就園蔬
見說高林外；樵人聽讀書

158 | WRITTEN IN ILLNESS

As I walk, I must rest every three steps;
The roof is leaking, I often change where I sit.
My wife tries protecting the tea cauldron;
A monk is able to provide funds for herbs!
In the neighbor's garden, the plum blossoms are all blooming;
Along the riverbank, plants are slow to grow.
Heaven understands poverty and illness,
But finds it hard to prevent my writing poetry.

病中作　　　　　　　　p. 15a

一行三步歇; 屋漏坐頻移
妻欲藏茶鼎; 僧能施藥資
鄰園梅盡發; 河岸草生遲
天解憐貧病; 難令不作詩

159 | THE CARRIAGE NOT TURNED BACK

Mountains and streams? Not so far away;
This wanderer hasn't turned his carriage.
I wish to speak of last night's dream,
But suddenly notice my book for this morning.
Singing birds are up on the roof;
Green plants grow in the courtyard.
Gazing up at the light of sun or moon,
I know they shine on you, dressed in court costume.

未迴車　　　　　　　pp. 14b–15a

山川匪遥遠; 行人未迴車
欲語昨宵夢; 忽接今朝書
啼鳥在屋上; 綠草生庭除
仰看日月光; 照知子衿裾

160 | MIDNIGHT

Midnight—alone, still lingering,
Wandering at leisure, gate still not shut.
On the stream-bank, mountains spit out the moon;
Rain dripping from the pines moistens my robe.
The echo of someone's skiff emerges, seems to draw closer;
Firefly glows gradually getting fewer.
What's not good is that affairs of the dusty realm
Often interfere with this feeling.

中夕   p. 15b

中夕獨依依；閒行未掩扉
水邊山出月；松上雨沾衣
棹響初如近；螢光漸欲稀
不甘塵內事；長與此心違

161 | INSCRIBED ON DING SHAOZHAN'S GARDEN VILLA

The district border lies beyond the low ridge;
I have come to this garden for a visit.
The path has changed since you planted new trees;
The hall is completed, though it has no name as yet.
Herb-sprouts have reached the height of grasses;
Streams from the cliff bring purity to your pond.
Would you know what are my feelings for you?
—Listen to a single cry of the crane from time to time.

題丁少瞻林園　　　　　　　p. 16a

州分低嶺外; 來向此園行
路改初栽樹; 堂成未有名
藥苗如草長; 巖溜入池清
欲識懷君意; 時聞鶴一鳴

162 | VISITING THE RESIDENCE OF A MONK

A visitor I come, no other agenda;
I never tire of knocking on your door.
These lovely mountains once hugged town walls;
Wrecked roofing is immediately rethatched.
Between serene tiles grow magic herbs;
The towering forest juts above distant suburbs.
The water-birds have mostly disappeared:
With spring warmth they're working on their nests.

訪僧居　　　　　　　p. 16a

客至無他事; 房門不厭敲
好山原帶郭; 損屋旋鋪茅
靜砌生靈藥; 高林出遠郊
水禽多不見; 春暖漸營巢

163 | THE TEMPLE OF ABILITY TO BE HUMANE

The temple has a stele telling its story;
It stands before the cliff of Guanyin.
The halls are high, lamp flames burning low;
Mountains close, chimes echo with rich tones.
The window is calm, cold snow blowing past;
Spring bird-calls follow the nighttime falls.
How can people know of this pure destination?
They say it's not the usual autumn scene.

能仁寺　　　　　　　p. 16b

寺置有碑傳; 觀音巖石前
殿高燈焰短; 山合磬聲圓
窗靜吹寒雪; 春鳴落夜泉
清遊人豈識; 謂不似秋天

164 | INSCRIBED ON LI SHANGSOU'S HALFWAY-VILLAGE CLIFF

One path, covered by green moss;
For years on end you've never left your gate.
Winds blow high—the pine trees sound with resonance;
The stream always full, the stones show no low-water marks.
Completely mindless of earning fame,
You make people feel your Way is noble.
Especially fearful lest an imperial summons arrive,
You move to another village still more remote.

題李商叟半村壁　　　　　　　　p. 16b

一徑蒼苔合; 連年不出門
風高松有韵; 溪滿石無痕
不自知名重; 令人覺道尊
更憂徵詔至; 移室向深村

165 | GIBBON HIDE

Along the road a Sichuan merchant
    selling a gibbon hide;
A single piece, all velvety,
    as if woven from black silk.
Often I use it as a cushion,
    seated by the window;
And then I think of when it was heard
    sadly crying in a hidden valley.
Killed by a crossbow! Suddenly I notice
    the wound can still be seen;
Sounds of flutes: who now boasts
    he can play upon the bones?
The ancient trees are clumped together,
    the road here twists and turns;
No one comes to write the poems
    of a rustic visitor.

猿皮　　　　　　　　　　　p. 18a

路逢巴客賣猿皮；一片蒙茸似黑絲
常向小窗鋪坐處；却思空谷聽啼時
弩傷忽見痕猶在；笛響誰誇骨可吹
古樹團團行路曲；無人來作野賓詩

166 | A Gathering with Drinking at the Pond-Pavilion of Inspector Bao

On your desk, just one lute,
    and several volumes of books;
At such a place, no need for singing
    to mouth-organ accompaniment.
Tired of living in the city
    and seeing so little of the sky,
Delighted to visit you in your home
    where I view so much of the moon.
Leaves cover the earth, and take off flying
    to follow the steps of your sandals;
The cranes are accustomed to human presence,
    and stay to hear chanting of poems.
Tomorrow morning again I will come
    to the mountains here,
Hands holding pine tree branches,
    nurturing Great Harmony.

會飲鮑使君池亭   p. 18b

案上一琴書數卷; 不須此處有笙歌
厭居城市觀天小; 喜到君家見月多
葉滿地飛隨步履; 鶴於人熟聽吟哦
明朝也向山中去; 手把松枝養太和

167 | VIEWING THE PURPLE MANDARIN DUCKS I AM RAISING

Whole bodies covered with patterning
    different from the ordinary,
And yet the leisure of their lives
    is not yet perfect freedom.
All day long by the blue-green hedge
    side by side they sleep:
Surely their souls must be dreaming together
    of flying to paradise!

觀所養鸂鶒   p. 20a

一身文采異常流; 却使閒身不自由
永日翠籬相並睡; 豈無魂夢到滄州

168 | INSCRIBED ON TRANSPORTATION OFFICIAL ZHAO'S BOAT-CABIN FOR CHANTING POEMS

It's difficult for flying dust
    to reach these azure waves,
Waves from which no two clouds
    ever look alike.
Done chanting poems, you don't realize
    you've startled the herons up:
Half the petals from their landspit
    land on your cabin-roof!

題趙運管吟篷   p. 20a

飛塵難到碧波中; 波上烟雲盡不同
吟斷不知驚鷺起; 汀花一半在船篷

169 | HEARING THE WATERS

Lamplight alone doesn't open
    the hearts of the travelers;
Suddenly we hear a cold roar
    sounding out like thunder.
There is no wind blowing,
    the trees are bare of leaves . . .
From Daozhou at midnight
    flood-waters are rushing by.

聞水   p. 20b

燈光難照客懷開; 忽聽寒聲響似雷
天氣無風樹無葉; 道州半夜水流來

170 | PRESENTED TO AN OLD MAN LIVING BY THE RIVER

Livelihood now passed on to your children,
You rise late, sun already high.
Basically no dusty affairs concern you;
White hairs have appeared at your temples.
From afar you get mountain-stream water to brew tea,
Recently transplanted thorn-bushes to patch the hedge.
Late in the day, you go off to do some fishing,
Your one dog following you as you leave.

贈溪上翁　　　　　　　pp. 35a–b

生事付諸兒；日高睡起遲
本無塵內事；亦有鬢邊絲
遠取泉烹茗；新移棘補籬
晚來持釣去；一犬自相隨

Drinking in the Moonlight, late 1100s–early 1200s. Ma Yuan (Ma Yüan 馬遠, c. 1150–after 1255), album leaf, ink on silk. The Cleveland Museum of Art, Bequest of Mrs. A. Dean Perry 1997.89. See poem 201 for Xu Ji's description of this agreeable pastime.

36 POEMS BY XU JI

(Lingyuan 靈淵, 1162–1214)

Page numbers refer to the one-chapter collected works of Xu Ji, "Poetry Collection from the Pavilion of the Double Ferns," (*Erweiting shiji* 二薇亭詩集) from the *Siku quanshu*.

171 | Sent to Yang Wanli

Your name exalted, your person also honored.
Yet you live in a little village, remote.
So pure your gateway seems like stream-water;
So poor gold glitters only from your sash.
You nurture your life, but not by eating herbs;
Your everyday conversation is of moral precepts,
Confucian scholar for the whole world!
We meet; I inquire about your news.

For Yang Wanli, see Introduction, p 12.

投楊誠齋   p. 3b

名高身又貴; 自住小村深
清得門如水; 貧惟帶有金
養生非藥餌; 常語是規箴
四海為儒者; 相逢問信音

172 | On a Winter's Day, Writing my Feelings

The courtyard's full of yellow leaves;
The garden trees form stark patterns.
Cold waters are pure blue all day;
The frosted sky turns red with evening.
I dine on vegetables, as if in a remote temple;
My thatched hut is near a friend down-stream.
It's not that I divide noise from silence:
From ancient times each has a beauty of its own.

冬日書懷   p. 4a

門庭黃葉滿; 園樹盡玲瓏
寒水終朝碧; 霜天向晚紅
蔬餐如野寺; 茅舍近溪翁
非是分囂寂; 由來趣不同

173 | On a Western Journey, Sent to my Three Friends, Weng, Zhao, and Xu

Late in winter, myself upon a journey:
Such the pain of my lowly office.
Crossing a river adds to my sadness;
Mountains I see make me miss my friends.
Mist arises late in this village;
Rain passes bamboo, pine trees, fresh.
Last night I dreamt of coming home:
I met you three—but oh! it wasn't real.

Dreaming of his friends is a testimonial to the bonds between Xu Ji and his fellow Four Lings.

西征有寄翁趙徐三友   p. 4b

窮冬逆旅身；薄宦此艱辛
渡水添愁思；看山憶故人
烟生村落晚；雨過竹松新
昨夜還鄉夢；逢君苦未真

174 | RISING AT DAWN

Dawn—I rise and wind blows my face;
Clear skies of morning, fogs disperse from fields.
I see the many towering peaks afar;
Few of the shallow streams are running slow.
Worldly affairs are not that hard to grasp,
It's only dusty labors that never cease.
This year I've seen change in temple hairs:
Already has appeared a strand of autumn.

晨起   p. 4b–5a

晨起風吹面; 朝晴野霧收
高峰多遠見; 淺水少平流
世事非難了; 塵勞獨未休
今年看鬢髮; 已見一莖秋

175 | XIANG RIVER

How many thousand li is Xiang River?
Smooth current, few rushing rapids.
Several households form villages or farms;
Rows of rocks rise into peaks and ridges.
Is it possible I've been here before?
No, I think I've seen it in a painting!
Chanting poems, I gradually age;
Now, here I will serve as a lowly official.

By the time of the Four Lings, "Eight Views of the Xiao and Xiang"
rivers (瀟湘八景) had become a widely popular subject in painting
and poetry (see poems 28, 73, and the following 176 and 177).
Here Xu Ji encounters a familiar scene on the Xiang River and
surmises he has seen it before in a painting.

湘水　　　　　　　　　p. 5a

湘水幾千里; 平流少急湍
數家分市井; 列石起峰巒
豈是昔曾到; 猶疑畫上看
吟詩身漸老; 向此作微官

176 | Mooring my Boat, Presented to Linghui

I moor my boat as wind again arises;
Tie the hawser to a forest of wild *wutong* trees.
The moon is blue in the skies of Chu;
Spring comes in, Xiang River waters deep.
The position is lowly, I yearn to be near the capital;
The place remote, feelings of homesickness rise.
What's good is that my fellow passengers
Are of pure character, and also love chanting poems.

Linghui is Xu Zhao of the Four Lings.

泊舟呈靈暉　　　　　pp. 5a–b

泊舟風又起; 繫纜野桐林
月在楚天碧; 春來湘水深
官貧思近闕; 地遠動愁心
所喜同舟者; 清贏亦好吟

177 | View from On High

On high I free my hermit's staff;
Green grasses fill the springtime slopes.
The wilds of Chu have no forests;
Mountains along the Xiang seem like waves.
My traveler's feelings change with the landscape;
Poetic thoughts are many once I leave my door.
And then there is the temple west of the river:
Sunset, and I still haven't visited there.

憑高　　　　　p. 5b

憑高散幽策; 綠草滿春坡
楚野無林木; 湘山似水波
客懷隨地改; 詩思出門多
尚有溪西寺; 斜陽未得過

178 | SELF-AWARENESS

I've studied the arts of "lightly leaping,"
And often feel wanderlust for ten thousand miles.
Over rivers and lakes the clouds seem like streams;
In the vastness of Ba the rocks look like forests.
Loving to drink, I'm always happy;
Saying nothing, my Way gains in depth.
The cinnabar Elixir is able to cure illness:
I'd never use it to turn lead into gold.

"LIghtly leaping" here seems to refer to techniques of mountain
climbing, or a type of stylized dance-like movements accompany-
ing certain rituals. Ba was the ancient state in what is now
eastern Sichuan.

自覺   pp. 6a–b

曾學輕騰術; 長懷萬里心
江湖雲似水; 巴廣石如林
好飲身常樂; 無言道更深
丹砂能愈疾; 不用化黃金

179 | INSCRIBED ON ATTENDANT CHEN'S LAKESIDE VILLA

The garden's less than three acres in extent,
But all four sides show water reaching sky.
Walk to the very highest spot
And you feel as if you're riding in a boat.
Wildflowers grow beyond the spring bank;
Mountain shapes stand beside ocean clouds.
Just let anyone come and visit here:
The feelings aroused are truly vast.

題陳待制湖莊　　　　　　p. 6b

園無三畝地; 四面水連天
行向樓高處; 却如身在船
野花春渚外; 山色海雲邊
一任人來往; 茲懷亦浩然

180 | Sent to Chen Xilao

For long days I've had no poet-companion;
In the calm courtyard I stand among nature's glories.
Bamboo branches slant down, moist with rain;
Plant colors, pure, invade sandy banks.
Of true spirit, my lifetime friend!
Here, neighbors, several tens of households.
Still I remember, inspired by light drunkenness
How I visited you for a cup of tea.

For the closeness of the Four Lings and Chen Xilao, see Weng
Juan's touching lament on the passing of Chen's mother (114).

寄陳西老　　　　　　　p. 6b

長日無吟伴；閒庭佇物華
竹枝斜帶雨；草色净侵沙
風度平生友；隣居幾十家
前曾乘小醉；訪爾一甌茶

181 | Happy that Monk Shi has Arrived

I live near a Buddhist monastery;
When they've time, monks come to ask of poetry.
This night among lakes and mountains in moonlight,
This season of chrysanthemums in dew!
Your words on Supreme Meaning always bring clarity;
Your soft chantings cause our steps to slow.
As I age, my friends grow fewer:
I love that you're still here as my companion.

As noted, Monk Shi seems to be a mutual friend of all Four Lings
(see 52, 90, and 92).

喜奭上人至　　　　　　　p. 7a

住與佛居近; 僧閒稍問詩
湖山明月夜; 風露菊花時
達意言常省; 微吟步自遲
老來朋舊少; 愛爾得相隨

182 | Dawn

My poet's temple-hairs all white at dawn;
A frosty sky seems clear as pure water.
Wind enters through chinks in the windows;
Ice forms in the pond of my inkstone.
Already growing gaunt, shadows of plum blossoms;
Still free of dew, bamboo leaves sound crisp.
Last night, Heaven and Earth were spotless;
All that remains, the light of the moon.

曉　　　　　　　　　pp. 7a–b

詩鬢曉星星; 霜天似水清
風當窗眼入; 冰向硯池生
已瘦梅花影; 猶乾竹葉聲
夜來天地潔; 惟是月華明

183 | SITTING ALONE, PRESENTED TO A GUEST

At dawn I rise, and again sit alone;
I draw stream water and brew myself some tea.
Cold mist adds to the color of bamboo;
Sparse snow, indistinguishable from the plum blossoms.
By myself, I enjoy forgetting worldly affairs;
What do they know of nature's changes of season?
Gentlemen! If you could only visit here,
The human realm would seem the home of Immortals.

孤坐呈客   pp. 8a–b

晨起猶孤坐; 缾泉自煮茶
寒烟添竹色; 疎雪亂梅花
獨喜忘時事; 誰知改歲華
多君能過此; 人裏似仙家

184 | INSCRIBED ON STONE GATE CAVE

Waterfall, crown of the southeast!
Even Mount Lu's cannot compare.
Flying down, it always seems to be raining;
The source from whence it flows is known to none.
In this cave, a dragon makes his home;
Along the stream, rocks form a gate.
Xie Lingyun practiced the Way here:
The foundation of his hut is still preserved.

Xie Lingyun (Hsieh Ling-yün 謝靈運, 385–433) was a famous poet of the Southern and Northern Dynasties and a lifelong practitioner of Buddhism.

題石門洞　　　　　　pp. 8b–9a

瀑水東南冠; 廬山未足論
飛來長似雨; 流處不知源
洞裏龍為宅; 溪邊石作門
修行謝康樂; 菴有故基存

185 | SPRING VIEW

From the tower I gaze at late spring;
Mist divides villages near and far.
With clear skies at dawn, thousands of trees, green;
After fresh rains half the pond muddy.
The willows are dense, warblers leave no shadows;
The mud is new, marks left by the swallows.
Light cold—my shirt-sleeves are too thin;
I pour out cups of wine, needing the warmth.

春望　　　　　　　　p. 9a

樓上看春晚; 烟分遠近村
曉晴千樹緑; 新雨半池渾
栁密鶯無影; 泥新燕有痕
輕寒衫袖薄; 杯酌更須温

186 | ON A SUMMER DAY VISITING A RECLUSE ON THE LAKE

Grueling heat—how can I escape?
In a solitary skiff I visit a recluse.
In this land of water, the lotus root is ripe;
Under clear skies, rice plants in the fields are fresh.
For study, I learn from the ancient masters;
Discussing Void I learn of my former lives.
Mirror Lake with its three hundred acres
Cannot compare to this lake's shores.

夏日湖上訪隱人　　　pp. 9b–10a

煩暑何能避; 孤舟訪隱人
水鄉菱藕熟; 晴野稻苗新
為學師前輩; 談空悟宿身
鏡湖三百頃; 不似此湖濱

187 | LIVING IN THE MOUNTAINS

Willows, bamboo hide an embankment of flowers;
Thatched roofs link with weedy ponds.
I open the door and startle up swallows;
Draw water, and get some baby fish.
The land is remote, still serene in spring;
Human life moves even slower here.
Mountain birds suddenly stop singing . . .
They fly up, then follow me ahead.

山居   p. 10a

栁竹藏花塢; 茅茨接草池
開門驚燕子; 汲水得魚兒
地僻春猶靜; 人閒日更遲
山禽啼忽住; 飛起又相隨

188 | ON A SUMMER DAY YEARNING FOR A POET-FRIEND

Flowing waters, calm, beneath the steps;
Sleeping alone I achieve freedom.
The moon arises, the wood approaches dawn;
Rain passes, the night feels like autumn.
From far I recall the bay of lotus blossom;
Who now chants poems about the bank of pollia flowers?
On such a fine night I fear I'll have no dream:
If I do, it will be a dream of us, wandering together.

夏日懷詩友   10a-b

流水堦除靜; 孤眠得自由
月生林欲曉; 雨過夜如秋
遠憶荷花浦; 誰吟杜若洲
良宵恐無夢; 有夢即俱遊

189 | INSCRIBED ON OLD MAN LI SHANG'S HALF-VILLAGE HALL

The place you live, half-linked to a village;
Your demeanor is entirely honorable.
If you're not welcoming fine guests,
Your bramble gate is kept closed at all times.
In search of verses, you walk the mountain shadows;
Wearing fisherman's coat you angle among patches of moonlight.
Staunch in poverty, eighty years of age,
One thing to count on: your name will be handed down.

題李商叟半村堂   p. 11b

住屋半依村; 先生氣象尊
若非迎好客; 長是掩柴門
覓句行山影; 披蓑釣月痕
固窮年八十; 惟得令名存

190 | CLIMBING TO SLANTWISE BLUE-GREEN VERANDAH–CONTINUING ZHAO CHANGFU'S POEM

Climbing step by step to the high, high temple,
Slowing walking—no need to be propped up.
The spring sky is clear, then rainy;
Mountain colors appear, then hide.
Poems I seek in the midst of this leisure;
Tea I call for after getting drunk.
What I regret is that our discussion was unresolved:
How about taking another trip up here?

登横碧軒繼趙昌甫作   p. 13b

步陟高高寺；徐行不用扶
春天晴又雨；山色有還無
句向閒中覓；茶因醉後呼
所懷論未足；何乃又征途

191 | ON THE RIVER

Ten days on the clear-water river,
New spring, skies of drizzling rain.
Green waves rise behind the sweep;
White birds sleep right near the boat.
Wheat plants as they start look just like grass;
Clouds are thick, yet half have turned to mist.
But I worry that the mountain roads are treacherous:
Tomorrow I must leave my river boat.

溪上   p. 13b–14a

十日清溪上；新春細雨天
綠波隨棹起；白鳥近舟眠
麥秀初如草；雲濃半是烟
却愁山路險；明日捨溪船

192 | In the Sixth Month, on the Way Home

Stars beam fading light from clear skies on the peaks;
The night is calm, I faintly hear the sound of flowing water.
In the sixth month, a traveler must be first to rise;
A skyful of chilly dew moistens his light robe.
Feelings of official duty fade along the road;
Lines of poems are mostly composed while seated on horseback.
All my friends back home must be imagining me
Surrounded by fragrance of rice plants, navigating my way home.

六月歸途   p. 15b

星明殘照數峰晴; 夜靜微聞水有聲
六月行人須早起; 一天涼露溼衣輕
宦情每向途中薄; 詩句多於馬上成
故里諸公應念我; 稻花香裏計歸程

193 | VISITING A FRIEND ON THE LAKE

In the city, day after day,
    I gaze at the southern lake,
Now I've begged time off so I
    can visit my hermit friend.
Gradually in the autumn showers
    chrysanthemums grow on the hedge;
As soon as the heat has dissipated,
    islet lotus, sparse.
The ancient paintings on the walls
    are mostly of wise sages;
The books that are piled on the desk
    are half of them Buddhist sutras.
I still haven't seen the master,
    but I do meet with his children:
Not knowing my surname and name
    they hesitate awkwardly.

訪湖友   pp. 15b–16a

城中日日望南湖；乞得閒來訪隱居
漸有秋霖籬菊長；纔無暑氣渚蓮疎
壁間古畫多賢像；案上塵編半佛書
未見主人逢稚子；不通姓字獨踟躕

194 | ON THE MID-AUTUMN FESTIVAL, WRITTEN AT A GATHERING AT THE TOWER OF BAO

Autumn day in a lakeside tower:
    the perfect place to spend it!
My little boat follows the lovely songs
    of the water-chestnut pickers.
Pale clouds veil the moon,
    making the whole sky white;
Distant waters give rise to coolness,
    increasing with the night.
It's already hard to find such sages
    to hold a gathering like this,
And how much the more so, on this Festival,
    a time for chanting poems.
Tomorrow morning, this will take place
    in the city of Xuancheng,
And folks will surely say, it was
    as elegant as Wang Xizhi's in the Yonghe time.

Wang Xizhi (Wang Hsi-chih 王羲之, 303–361 CE) was a scholar, politician, and general active during the Yonghe period (345–6) of the Jin Dynasty, and regarded by some as China's greatest calligrapher.

中秋集鮑樓作　　　　　　　16a

秋在湖樓正可過；扁舟窈窕逐菱歌
淡雲遮月連天白；遠水生涼入夜多
已是高人難會聚；矧逢佳節共吟哦
明朝此集喧城市；應說風流似永和

195 | Presented to Zhao Shixiu

The wandering official has come back home,
    after—how many springs?
Gaunt and pure, still he presents
    the same person as before.
You've nurtured mind and nature,
    so only now can you be calm;
You've converted wife and children,
    so they don't whine, "We're so poor!"
The bamboo's tall, its fresh shadiness
    seems deep, just like a cave;
The plum trees have added strange formations,
    older than those who view them.
I also know that you have met
    with men of reputation:
Your recent compositions have
    a power equal to theirs.

贈趙師秀   p. 16b

遊宦歸來隔幾春; 清羸還是舊時身
養成心性方能靜; 化得妻兒不說貧
竹長新陰深似洞; 梅添怪相老於人
亦知曾見高人了; 近作文章氣力勻

196 | PRESENTED TO XU ZHAO

Recently you've practiced the Perfect Awareness:
    What is this new realm like?
It's like the moon, cold, high in void,
    shadows thrown on waves.
Your body? Strong! And that's because
    you've eaten few cooked dishes;
Your poetry? Pure! And that derives
    drinking lots of tea.
Living in town to you is like
    living in mountains, calm;
Your dreams at night are utterly free
    of the worldly Anxiety-Demon.
Yesterday you must have come
    to the front gate of my home:
I know, as I traced your crane-like footsteps,
    dancing on the green sedge.

贈徐照　　　　　　pp. 16b–17a

近參圓覺境如何；月冷高空影在波
身健却緣餐飯少；詩清都為飲茶多
城居亦似山中靜；夜夢俱無世慮魔
昨日曾知到門外；因隨鶴步踏青莎

197 | DESCRIBING MATTERS OF EARLY SPRING

You emerge from your gate, walking calmly,
    flora flourishing richly;
In the shade of mulberry trees
    are also worn footpaths.
In clear-sky mist through so many trees,
    warblers are singing early;
Over the whole pond of springtime waters
    swallows are darting low.
Like Tao Yuanming, in vain you took
    the office of magistrate;
Hard to emulate Yan Ling and live
    right along the stream-side.
In this Enlightened Regime you've benefited
    by the taint of low salary:
Unable to suffer this kind of life,
    again you climb to high places.

Yan Ling was a fisherman tapped by a ruler as his advisor,
but later returned to his simple fisherman's life. This could be
addressed to Zhao Shixiu who, along with Xu Ji himself, were
the only two of Four Lings to serve in government, and that
on a low level.

新春書事   p. 17a

出門閒步草萋萋; 桑柘陰中亦有蹊
幾樹晴烟鶯囀早; 一塘春水燕飛低
空如陶亮官為令; 難學嚴陵住近溪
聖世幸時沾薄禄; 不能辛苦又攀躋

199 | INSCRIBED ON THE STUDIO FOR NURTURING CLUMSINESS

When Chaos divided and the world emerged,
    things evolved to the present;
In great profusion, clever dealings
    grew into a jungle.
The moon may be bright, but can't avoid
    the Frog Monster devouring a part;
At the Autumn Solstice, just as before,
    crickets are chattering away.
And I lament my entire life
    is nothing but delusion;
Who can avoid the ten thousand affairs
    so they won't involve his mind?
But coming to your study, sir,
    it's pure as mountain water—
You must have caused all vulgar machinations
    to desist from their invasion.

Line three offers a folk explanation for the eclipse of the moon.

題養拙齋   pp. 17a–b

混沌分來便至今；紛紛巧事日成林
月明未免蝦蟇食；秋至依然蟋蟀吟
自嘆一身全是幻；誰能萬事不容心
到君齋舍清如水；應使凡機盡弗侵

200 | STOPPING AT MASTER MA'S RIDGE

I tie up my boat as dawn appears,
  and walk on level sand;
By evening I stop among the cloud-roots,
  the first house encountered there.
Newly gathering vegetables
  are moist with country dew;
And too he's built a sturdy hedge
  to carry mountain flowers.
Before his gate and facing him,
  green peaks, rather small;
Behind his house, flowing forth,
  a white-water streams slants by.
How loveable! This mountain dweller
  has nothing else to do
But, west of the vine-woven enclosure,
  to watch the swarms of bees.

"Cloud-roots" refers to mountain rocks, from which clouds were believed to emerge.

泊馬公嶺   p. 17b

維舟拂曉步平沙; 晚泊雲根第一家
新取菜蔬沾野露; 旋編籬落帶山花
門前相對青峰小; 屋後流來白水斜
可愛山翁無一事; 藤牆西畔看蜂衙

201 | WINE

I've just poured out a brimming cupful—
    azure and perfectly pure!
It was brewed by my mountain wife,
    her own technique, her hands.
"Don't let the water be too much,
    to prevent too thin a taste;
You must be sure the wine-mold's sparse
    to get the perfect scent."
Coolness rises from the breezes
    blowing through the lotus;
Warmth is born from plum blossoms,
    bathed in the moonlight.
Worldly flavors simply lack
    a taste like this one—
Who deeply understands this flavor?
    Only Tao Yuanming.

The last line refers again to the famous scholar-recluse (see 10, 81, and 197).

酒　　　　　　pp. 17b–18a

才傾一盞碧澄澄；自是山妻手法成
不遣水多防味薄；要令麴少得香清
涼從荷葉風邊起；暖向梅花月裏生
世味總無如此味；深知此味即淵明

202 | PASSING BY NINEFOLD RIDGE

Sheer cliffs, steep roads,
    water flowing fast,
I ride down to the mountain's base,
    then climb another mountain.
My vision takes in further peaks
    arising from the clouds,
Unaware that my body too
    is enfolded by the clouds.

過九嶺　　　　　　　　　　p. 19a

斷崖橫路水潺潺; 行到山根又上山
眼看別峰雲霧起; 不知身也在雲間

203 | INSCRIBED ON CHEN XILAO'S PAINTING, *MOUNTAINS OF SHU*

Standing like walls, the green mountains
    flank narrow streams;
Serene clouds all day long
    naturally rise, then dip.
Realizing how far the forest
    of spring trees reaches back,
There must be pure-voiced gibbons there,
    singing their sad songs.

Shu is an ancient name for what is now roughly Sichuan province. In this case the poet openly states that he is *surmising* the presence of sound, an interesting variation on the ekphrastic and synaesthetic formula by which sounds are attributed to paintings.

題陳西老畫蜀山圖　　　　pp. 19a–b

壁立青山帶峽溪; 閒雲盡日自高低
知他春樹深多少; 應有清猿在裏啼

204 | THE TOWER OF PAINTING

Blue-green mist, rain from nowhere,
    suddenly appear, then disappear;
Who created this masterpiece
    with the tip of a brush?
Streams and mountains here have been
    painted by a person;
And yet we say "These streams and mountains
    seem just like a painting!"

丹青閣   p. 20a

翠靄空霏忽有無; 筆端誰著此工夫
溪山本被人圖畫; 却道溪山是畫圖

205 | THE START OF AUTUMN

The start of autumn—a single rainfall
    washes clean forests and passes;
Evening colors are pure and fresh,
    filling the panorama.
The wind is gentle—white clouds move
    laterally without a break,
And in front of the mountains give form to
    a new layer of mountains.

新秋   22a

新秋一雨洗林關; 晚色清澄滿望間
風靜白雲橫不斷; 山前又疊一重山

206 | THE TEMPLE OF FLOURISHING PEAKS

My palanquin at evening stops
    beside a cliffside cavern;
This monastery entrance opens on
    an ancient avenue.
The monks come out to greet me,
    and then they recognize me:
In ten years I have made three visits
    to the Temple of Flourishing Peaks.

秀峰寺   p. 23a

籃輿晚歇近岩隈; 精舍門臨古道開
僧子相逢便相識; 十年三過秀峰來

FLOATING WORLD EDITIONS publishes books that contribute to a deeper understanding of Asian cultures. Editorial supervision: Ray Furse. Book and cover design: Liz Trovato. Printing and binding: IngramSpark. The typefaces used are: Cormorant Garamond, Anavio, and SongTi.

Printed in the USA
CPSIA information can be obtained
at www.ICGtesting.com
CBHW062229090624
9826CB00008B/84

9 781953 225054